Divine Antlervention

AMAZING TRUE STORIES OF THE BIG ONE'S THAT GOT AWAY!

(and the *INCREDIBLE* circumstances that caused it)

To Shelly, Theny & Shawn -
Enjoy, your friend,
Dave Panetti

Dave Panetti

Divine Antlervention

Copyright 2011 by David F. Panetti. All rights reserved.

No part of this publication may be reproduced, stored in a retrieval system or transmitted in any way, by any means, without the prior written permission of the author except as provided by USA copyright law.

ISBN 978-0-615-50418-6

BIG BUCK BOOK PUBLISHING CO.
PANAMA CITY BEACH, FLORIDA

To order more books or future titles by this author, please go to: **bigbuckbooks.com**

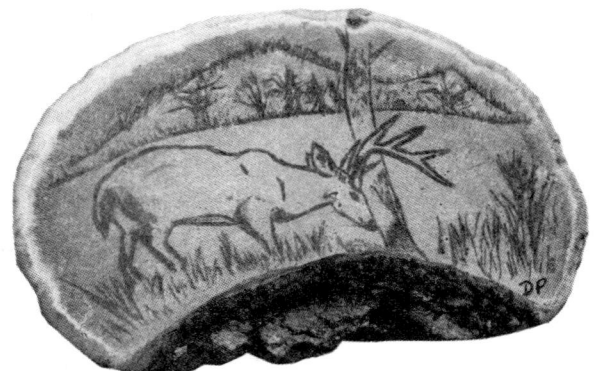

About the Author

According to Dave Panetti, he's convinced he was born a few hundred years too late. His ideal life would have been living in the woods somewhere amongst the Native American Indians, either chasing Buffalo on horseback or stalking Whitetail Deer and Antelope on foot with a bow and arrow.

Growing up in the Northeast, the forest was Dave's home away from home, and the wildlife that lived there was his obsession. Spending countless hours observing every critter with fur or feathers advanced to *bringing home* every critter as his new pet! Baby raccoons and possums were common, with the possibility of *any* distressed animal wandering in for some temporary assistance. This habit continues today as he takes care of abandoned dogs, exotic birds, fish, and yes...a bedraggled stray turkey named "Turkulees!"

On the other hand, being a passionate bowhunter, Dave lives to bowhunt and has taken multiple numbers of many species of North American Big Game over the years that qualify for the Pope and Young *and* the coveted Boone and Crockett record books. Dave feels, "More important than the outcome of a hunt is the experience of the hunt." This requires nothing more than a little extra awareness of your surroundings and pays huge dividends to the conscience of mind. He believes, *"Actually getting something is a bonus to the hunt!"*

This extra awareness has led to the recognition, or realization of the recurring phenomenon known as *"Divine Antlervention."* In fact, it has happened to him so many times, you could say, *"He wrote the book on it!"*

Dave currently lives on the Gulf Coast of Florida- saltwater fishing being his other passion. He enjoys the beach, boating, reading, writing music on the guitar and piano, high definition wood carving, gardening, and gourmet cooking with a good glass of wine!

About the Artist

Steve Close is a graduate of Troy State University with a BS in Art Education. This has led Close through a twenty-five year career as an art educator, instructing students from kindergarten through adults in the realm of all art mediums.

Close's work can be found in many private collections and limited edition prints have been created from many of his paintings. These include historical images for the LaGrange Chamber of Commerce and Okeechobee Chamber of Commerce. A set of four images for Hills and Dales and an old fashioned St. Nicolas image that was included in the Neiman Marcus Christmas Catalogue.

Steve Close works in various drawing media, including water color and acrylic. He enjoys the spontaneity of plein air painting, focusing on the compositions and values of light seen in nature. He often takes those studies back to the studio to explore the abstraction of nature through shape and color.

"Being an art educator for over thirty years has helped me develop an appreciation for various styles of art. I find abstract to tightly rendered illustrations to be inspiring if the work has the "wow" factor. That "wow" factor is what I'm constantly trying to create and that is what keeps me painting. Currently, I am trying to create recognizable images that have a combination of recognizable subject matter and interest in the surface of the painting."

Close continues to teach and reside in LaGrange, Georgia with his wife, Donna, when he is not painting at his family's Highland, North Carolina home.

For more information about obtaining signed, numbered prints of the illustrations included in this book and other art work by Close, please contact Steve at: closesc123@gmail.com

Special Thanks and Acknowledgements

I would like to thank my editors, Nancy Walker and Bill McCandliss for their generous efforts on this project. The countless hours spent with me was an education I could have only received in college classes. I appreciate every minute of it, "Thank you very much!"

I would also like to thank the landowners who have allowed me to share their land and enjoy something that is very important and sacred to me...my time in the woods.

My artist, Steve Close, deserves great praise for taking the time to "get inside" each story to understand the significance and reason for the design of each drawing as they pertain to the story. Each drawing puts me right back in the moment...great job Steve! (See "About the Artist" for more information and how to obtain any of his signed artwork.)

Introduction

Has this happened to you? With no pun intended, I'll bet you a hundred *"**bucks**"* it has! The moment you've waited your whole hunting life for is suddenly here. With little warning, he suddenly appears and is heading in your direction. He has no idea you're there...the wind is in your favor. Finally, you're going to get a chance at that,"Once in a lifetime" monster buck of your dreams!

At just 20 yards, with your heart pounding right through all the layers of camouflage clothing, you draw back your bow, take aim, and...*it happens!*

The arrow falls off the string and goes "Ping, pang, ping," as it hits every tree branch on the way to the ground. The buck instantly swaps ends, running full speed in the opposite direction, waving his flag- not to surrender, but to remind you why he's named the Whitetail Deer!

In the following moments of disarray, it's over as quickly as it began, leaving you desperately speechless as he melts back into the depths of the forest, never to be seen again.

Did that really just happen? "Why me, why right now?" you ask yourself. A simple error like that hasn't happened since you were a little kid! But, to rival all other blunders, it just did. Years of diligent practice and untold preparation means nothing now. While scratching your head in a state of total confusion, you question your belief in mere coincidences. The woods return to an eerie silence as the only sound remaining is the rapid beating of your newly broken heart.

Allow me explain: First of all, you're not alone. This was nobody's fault and you had nothing to do with it. That's right, *out of your hands!*

You see, there's a phenomenon in nature that occurs only when that trophy of a lifetime is finally right there in front of you for the taking. It mysteriously appears out of nowhere, and causes everything to go inexplicably wrong at the moment of truth. Every hunter I know is familiar with this situation, and for some, all *too* familiar. I can personally vouch for hundreds of these occurrences in my lifetime. It keeps the biggest antlered animals from becoming wallhangings, and keeps us humbled hunters coming back year after year for another round of nature's ultimate *"game!"*

The arrow story above is a simplified example of what I'm about to share with you. The following chapters are far more unbelievable, yet incredibly- ***100% true!*** The stories go from mild to wild, and will leave you wondering, *"Could this really be possible?"* Only to be confirmed by your personal recollections, as it has happened on more than one occasion in your own neck of the woods.

It's Nature's Guardian Angel, the ever lurking phenomenon known as...*"Divine Antlervention!"*

CONTENTS

A NIGHTMARE IN ANGELFIRE
13

WHAT BIG EYES YOU HAVE!
29

SOME OF THE BEST HUNTS START OUT THIS WAY!
39

TIMING IS EVERYTHING
49

ALASKAN DREAM HUNT
55

THIRD TIMES' A CHARM! (or is it)?
61

THE EARLY WARNING SIGNS
69

NOW YOU SEE IT!
79

IT COMES IN MANY FORMS
85

INVISIBLE
89

MISGUIDED
93

THE BUCK STOPS HERE
97

SO CLOSE, YET SO...*CLOSE!*
101

A WILD MOOSE CHASE
(The Tale of the Bull)
105

IN FACT...STRANGER THAN FICTION!
113

CONCLUSION AND FINAL THOUGHTS
117

A NIGHTMARE IN ANGEL FIRE

*I*f you're like most people that live to deer hunt, you'll absolutely love elk hunting as well. If you've ever been out west and visited the Rocky Mountains, you'll know why. States like Colorado, Wyoming, Idaho, and Montana, well...it just doesn't get any better than that! Mother Nature showcase's her finest work there.

My personal favorite elk hunting state happens to be New Mexico. Not just because the elk are big, and occasionally you can *win the lottery* and draw a "High Demand" bull tag...its because they have "Green Chiles!" I love Green Chiles! Whenever you go to a restaurant, the question the waitress always asks is, "Red or Green?" My answer is always, "Yes and yes!" In New Mexico, they put chile on everything! Eggs, cheeseburgers, spaghetti, you name it. They even put chile on their chilli!

The other reason of course, is the elk. Big bulls can be found in almost any hunting unit in the state and I've bowhunted many of them to safely make that claim. One year a friend of mine shot a bull in one of the Gila units we were hunting, that we rough scored in camp and the grand tally turned out to be a whopping 406 inches! This bull just walked right up to him on the first afternoon of our hunt, stopped at 20 yards, raked his antlers on the ground as he went through his rutting ritual, stood there and let my buddy shoot him while he video taped the whole thing! That kind of luck just doesn't happen for me...and I took this person on his first elk hunt just a couple years earlier got him get his first elk! They say, "No good deed goes unpunished," but this was ridiculous. Nonetheless, I was very proud, as my friend has become one of the best elk hunters I've known to this day.

Rewinding the tape back a couple of years, I often hunted in Northern New Mexico near the ski resort town of Angel Fire. The elk hunting is superb and the scenery is as picturesque as a post card! I also have some good friends that live in the area. Occasionally, we would take a day off from elk hunting, rent a boat at Eaglenest Lake, and fish for landlocked salmon and rainbow trout. The fresh salmon were especially delicious grilled...served with a little Green Chile of course!

An old friend of mine who lives in Angel Fire told me about an area to hunt, off the beaten path and out in the middle of nowhere. The only way to access the area was with four-wheel drive vehicles and Warn wenches attached. It was uphill most of the way until you got to the mud bogs near the top. We always took two trucks because one would inevitably get stuck in the knee-deep muck and we needed the other truck to pull it out every time!

In spite of the difficulty reaching our destination, when we eventually arrived, we were in elk heaven...or heaven itself! It was incredibly beautiful in that expansive, flowery meadow surrounded by towering mountains, which made all the effort getting there worthwhile.

In the evening, the elk would come down the mountain draws and bugle at the camper all night long. The graceful multi-note whistle of a bull elk is music to anyone's ears. However, if a person wanted to sleep, earplugs were mandatory! In the morning, you'd have to sneak past the elk in the dark to get the top of the mountain ahead of them to hunt effectively. This backward logic always puzzled me for some reason.

Usually, my first choice was to take a friend who had never elk hunted before and show him the incredible beauty of the area, and of elk hunting itself. I simply enjoyed doing all the calling, while letting them do all the shooting. To me, calling was the fun part. The expression on their faces when that first mature bull would come in to bow range-tearing trees apart with angry steam bellowing from each nostril, and bugle from only yards away was worth the price of admission!

After a few days of *buddy hunting*, my compadres were all well versed enough to hunt by themselves or with each other. At this time, I generally like to sneak off on my own and seek out a monster bull. I also love the peaceful solitude of being alone in the woods, most of all.

Often, I would wander great distances, calling and listening to locate that one exceptional bull I was after. If you hunt elk long enough, you'll learn to match the size of an elk to his bugle, and sometimes, a unique bugle to a particular elk. The story of "The Screamer" starts here!

On one of my solo adventures one afternoon, I decided to take a break and rest for a while. Along the edge of a beautiful mountain top meadow, I settled in at the base of a extremely tall Ponderosa Pine tree for an early afternoon catnap. I always looked forward to that time of the day, when the sound of the westerly winds wisp through the pine needles overhead, and the intense, deep sleep that occurs in such places as that.

While dreaming of whistling bulls, I was suddenly awakened by one such sound. It startled me! I wondered, did I just hear that or was it a psychosomatic reaction in my state of *"sound sleep?"* Either way, I was now sitting straight up and on full alert!

Confirmation of the distant bugle I thought I heard came in just seconds later. Then, another blast and another as the bull was heading toward the meadow I was surveying. A quick assessment of the wind told me I was on the wrong side of the park and I better get a move on.

Cows and calves were now mewing as they entered the meadow. I had to quickly back out of the area and circle downwind to avoid detection. Consequently, I had to trek all the way around the meadow's perimeter get closer to where the elk were now feeding.

As I closed in from the northeast corner of the park, there was no problem keeping tabs on the bull's whereabouts. The big herd bull never stopped bugling. That would become his trademark. Then, he emerged into the opening and promptly destroyed a pine sapling. What a first impression!

He was a massive-bodied bull with a rack that would command instant respect from all other elk in the area. He had an attitude to match! His shrill, high-pitched whistle descended to deeper, angrier tones, ending with a furious guttural growl and a series of chuckles as if to ask, "Got any questions?" No bull could match his confidence and no cows would ever attempt to stray from the herd. If one did, he would take off after her like an over-controlling Border Collie. And with his sharp, ivory-tipped antlers, a few painful, scolding jabs to her posterior would round her back up into his harem.

The herd kept moving away in the opposite direction. No verbal imitation I could produce would pull this "big boy" away from the ladies, not even with my favorite triple reed diaphragm that was personally given to me by Will Primos at a local convenience store in the village of Angel Fire during this trip.

Since there was plenty of time left on my hunt, I opted to let the herd continue on. I was somewhat sure of the location of their bedding area, and *very* sure this seven by seven, 370 inch thoroughbred was the one I would focus all my attention on.

Back in camp that evening, I told the guys of this great find. Everyone was excited for me and could hardly wait to see what would happen next. I asked everyone to please stay out of that particular area and let me see what I could do with this bull, undisturbed. All agreed since they were my friends and guests and they knew I would gladly take them out hunting anytime- *and do all the calling for them!*

The following day, I was back in the meadow patiently waiting. Prime time couldn't come soon enough and hopefully my vocal bull would be repeating his routine. I was repeating *mine* with another nap under the same Ponderosa Pine tree!

Early that afternoon, a thunderstorm blew in unexpectedly from the Northwest. It rumbled with a vengeance! The wind picked up and the cold rain came pouring down on a near horizontal angle. "No problem," I thought. I always carried a rain jacket, and decided to wait it out. Then, the lightning bolts came crashing down! I was no stranger to this kind of weather, since I live in the "lightning state" of Florida, statistically, the most lethal. Needless to say, *I was out of there!*

I didn't get more than forty yards away from that big ol' Ponderosa Pine when the loudest explosion I've ever heard went off right behind me! Lightning hit the big tree and I hit the ground as every hair stood straight up while I dug in for cover. Voltage seemed to shoot through my body, (although I'm quite sure it was just a natural reaction to *human* shock!) Chunks of steaming wood flew over my head and landed all around me. I looked back to see what had just happened, and the big Ponderosa Pine was annihilated on contact! It continued smoldering and I continued shaking...thinking, "Wasn't I just sitting at the base of that tree...sound asleep?"

Later in the day, the storm had passed and I could still hear the distant rumbles getting further away. True to form, at exactly the same time and location as the previous day, the first of many Wapiti sirens went off. It was *him*. Like I said earlier in the story, you can sometimes match a certain bugle to a particular bull, this one was a no brainer!

At 4:15 in the afternoon, I was already in position with the wind in my favor. "The Screamer" was working in my direction. As I backed into a large brush pile, I nocked an arrow and waited as the sounds got closer and closer. Bugle after bugle, the anticipation was killing me. Coming to me like he was on a string, he moved his cows to within a hundred yards or so when I heard another bugle come from behind me. I thought, I'll just let this other bull do what he's going to do. I wasn't interested in him anyway. Then the new comer bugled again. Then again, and again until I realized the quality of the sound was a little substandard. Of all the luck, it was another hunter! Way up here, I thought?

The Screamer stopped screaming, but the impostor continued *impostering*. The more he called, the worse it sounded, and the whole herd retreated to the other side of the Rocky Mountains.

I broke out my favorite triple reed and blew a few notes. The other hunter bugled right back and moved in closer. I bugled one more time, and again he came closer until I called him right in to the other side of the brush pile I was hiding in. A rude shock set in when I recognized it to be one of the fellows in my own camp! Remaining quiet, I clearly saw who it was, as I did just call him into easy bow-range. I still had an arrow nocked, but quickly extinguished that thought!

This friend never did see me. I guess he assumed the bull just lost interest and left the area...then, so did the "claim jumper." I never heard another peep out of my big bull that evening, but I was determined he and I would meet again.

Later that night in camp was very awkward, because I wasn't sure how to address the problem to the offender. I have never had a hunt foiled in *this* manner before. Being too upset for words myself, my life long buddy Chris Lorea from Montana addressed the issue for me. He delivered a verbal laceration based on the one and only request I had asked of my guests. Afterwards, we had a clear understanding and a very peaceful camp. Chris handled it better than I could have and I thanked him for that. (I guess Chris noticed I still hadn't put the arrow back in the quiver!)

A couple days later, I relocated the bull working in a whole new area, miles away from his primary park where I had originally found him. At least he was still in the same hunting unit! His voice easily gave him away, but I felt like I was starting from scratch all over again.

My hope was rekindled as I watched him corral his harem into a new meadow. I noticed he had picked up a few new girlfriends along the way without sacrificing any headgear. Observing his behavior, there seemed to be one chink in his armor. He liked to do things repetitively, as long as he wasn't disturbed in the process. My idea was to hunt him like I would hunt a whitetail deer. I now knew exactly what he was doing...where and when. Tomorrow, all he had to do was follow today's footsteps.

The next day, I was literally hunting his entry trail to the new park. Being a whitetail hunter, this was simple logic to me, but not your standard method for elk. Would he follow the script?

Sure enough, I could have set my watch to them because it was again 4:15 in the afternoon and here they came. The freight train-bugles echoed through the pine forest right on schedule. I felt like I was somehow cheating at the game, as one cow after another passed on the upwind side of the trail. "How easy does this get?" I slyly smirked. The bull's ivory tipped rack reminded me of a tree all lit up for the holidays, and approaching fast. It looked like Christmas was coming early!

At 25 yards, it was time to close the deal. I slowly drew back my compound bow as he stepped behind a large sapling. "This is it," I thought, and the moment I got to full draw...the bow exploded in my hands! That's right, **"K-POW!"** Parts flew everywhere!

The woods erupted, sounding like a cattle drive going through the forest heading to Pie Town! Branches were breaking, logs were snapping, elk were literally running everywhere. Was I (a) Confused? (b) Upset? (c) Inventing new words? Or, (d) All the above? ...***Correct!***

Soon thereafter, the archery season ended. I went home feeling bamboozled! Was this the mystifying phenomenon at its finest, I wondered? Not by a long shot! I planned to return next year to the same area, hoping to find the same bull having survived the rifle season and the harsh winter as you would expect in a ski resort town such as Angel Fire.

The following archery elk season finally opened, and the first area to try to locate "Mr. Fortunate" was the original meadow he used the previous year as his preferred stomping grounds.

The first afternoon of the hunt produced a repeat performance of the previous year, as though we never skipped a beat. "The Screamer" was still out there, I was thrilled! Screaming through the woods, bugle after bugle, he pushed the cows away from the bedding area. This time however, entering into a different corner of the park, it left me far out of position to put a move on him. The wind was completely wrong. So, I backed out of the area, but not before closely monitoring his every move to determine how he was getting to that corner of the park, which I hadn't been to before.

There was something very unusual when they got there. I could not see any of the elk. No doubt they were there, and it was him screaming away and tearing up trees. I just couldn't see them! Granted, they were a couple hundred yards away, but "Where were all the elk?"

They hung around that southwest corner for a long time, raising all kinds of ruckus. Then it got too dark and I had a long haul back to camp. I thought, "Is this year going to be just like last year? Am I going to be jinxed all over again? Would the next day be *my* day, or is this big bull just arrow proof?" I wanted to know if that could be possible, and was willing to bet my whole hunt on finding out.

Again, this is year two on the same bull. I figured by the sound of his roar and the havoc he wreaked on those poor little pine saplings, he must be *HUGE* by now. I couldn't wait to see the rack he must have grown during this summer. It had to be over 390 inches by now, I figured.

Upon awakening the next day, I had no interest in the morning hunt as I had a solid game plan for the afternoon. I had a date with fate, and this time I had high expectations of changing my unlucky streak.

Instead, I opted to take my good buddy, Marvin Blackburn from Paso Robles, California with me to an area I ran across while trying to locate my chosen bull. I had found lots of elk in the area, and Marvin jumped on the opportunity to go on a *guided* hunt with me doing all the calling for him.

Marvin and his brother Greg were two of the funniest guys you would ever want to meet. Their stories in camp kept us all in stitches, from the time they woke up in the morning, to the wee hours of the last glowing ambers in the campfire. I'm surprised their last name isn't Foxworthy!

After a long hike, we arrived at my secret location and set up to call. The first bull of the day answered from a few hundred yards away as we rearranged our setup to correct the wind. I placed Marvin out ahead of me about 20 yards, in front of a patch of small trees and thickets. I continued calling with some sultry cow calls, followed by a couple lost calf calls.

The bull was just over the hill. He must have been excited because he was coming fast, closing the gap between us in a matter of seconds! I motioned to Marvin to get ready. We could hear twigs snapping and branches cracking under each approaching footstep. Bows in hand, arrows on the string, we were in perfect position. Just a few more steps and the bull would appear right in front of us, but he didn't...

Instead, a four-hundred and fifty pound cinnamon colored Black Bear did!!! At just 20 yards, he was heading straight for Marvin! "Holy ! @*#!" I thought. This could really get ugly now, as the bear was only 10 yards from him! I could see the beads of sweat and an expression of fear on Marvin's camouflage face. This was not what we bargained for and this was no ordinary bear. He was a big, hungry boar looking for that one carnivorous meal before hibernation, and just by being there, we willingly entered the food chain!

The monster bruin stopped and stared into the brush pile in front of him. He knew something wasn't right. Marvin held his ground and remained motionless. Then the bear turned his head to the right, looked directly at me...***and charged!***

Before I could react, the bear hit me and knocked me on my...as I was saying, head over teakettle, as my bow and I went tumbling! I landed five feet away, lying face down on the ground with a big "Grizzly" looking bear standing over me! His head was so close to mine I could feel his breath hitting me on the side of my face, and it didn't smell like Listerine. I attempted to keep a lid on my fear and didn't dare move as I wondered how I was ever going to get out of this one? How was it going to feel when those big canine teeth punctured through the back of my skull with one powerful bite! How would it feel to be eviscerated alive? Either way, I predicted pain, and thought, "What a way to go...I knew it would end like this someday!" With all the time I spend in the woods, it had to! But, why me? Why would *Marvin* get to watch while *I* got eaten? The bear saw *him* first, didn't he?

Appropriately, I said my prayers for the first time in longer than I care to admit, but it must have worked. I noticed the bear was looking around the woods as I wrenched my eyeballs as far to the right as humanly possible without moving my head. Then, the instant our eyes met, the bears teeth flared and he lounged at my face but missed as I instantly buried my head in the ground, face down.

Cold chills ran through me as I realized eye contact could have been a fatal mistake! Vowing not to move a muscle, I fought off the reaction to shiver involuntarily. Time stood still as I waited for the worst...and waited...and waited. Then slowly, the bear eased off of me and took one last look around. Then, he suddenly dashed off, running down the hill, crashing through whatever was in his way!

I guess the bear didn't like the way I smelled either. Then all of a sudden, for some strange reason...*neither did I!*

I got to my knees and looked for Marvin. He came running over and said, "Dave, are you all right? Are you OK?" I gathered a deep breath, exhaled, and said, "...Well, you're a big help!" Apologizing, Marvin had done exactly the right thing...which was nothing! We both knew one false move and it would have been all over for me. "That was the wildest thing that has ever happened to me in the woods ...*ever!*" I said. Marvin and I had no choice but to laugh out loud in euphoric relief! "Can you believe what just happened?" "No one back in camp is going to believe us, or anyone else in the world, for that matter!" However, we were each other's witnesses, and we knew we'd always have that to back our story.

We took a few minutes to gather our thoughts, and again, my bow parts. Thankful to be alive, we decided to head back toward camp. Shaking our heads in astonishment, we hadn't gone a couple hundred yards, when I spotted a lone bull feeding up ahead in a small meadow. He wasn't a big bull by any means, but Marvin had never shot an elk before and wanted me to call this one in for him. We got set up in one minute or less. I put Marvin 40 yards out ahead of me again and began calling right away.

The young bull was very agreeable and coming straight in, but I was too busy looking around for bears! This bull came closer and closer. He came so close to Marvin that he had no shot; the bull was facing forward. I had to turn him a little to get a better angle for Marvin to shoot or the bull would run right into him. A soft cow call blown over my shoulder and off to the right did the trick as the bull turned and walked broadside at ten yards. Marvin shot, and the bull went down. His first elk, and just minutes before, we were being attacked by a giant bear! What a day this has been!

The day wasn't over yet. I still had an afternoon appointment with the Screamer. After packing out elk meat, I showered, changed camos and returned to the meadow for the afternoon hunt.

Without any time for the afternoon nap that I now *truly* needed, I had some fast scouting to do. I wanted to know why I couldn't see the elk entering the park the night before when they were right there in front of me. I didn't have much time to figure it out.

Noticing that at the end of the park, the last one hundred yards or so of clearing took a small turn to the left and was hidden by woods. It also declined steeply downhill until it reached more woods. Just below the top of the hill was a flat shelf which contained a large wallow. I had my answer! This was why I couldn't see any elk the night before. They were all at this wallow just below my line of sight. I was thrilled with this new discovery!

I decided to build a makeshift ground blind at the edge of the woods just downwind of the wallow, but it had to be done quickly. The magic hour was rapidly approaching and I had plenty of work to do.

The blind was completed in record time and the trap was set. Next, all that the elk had to do was show up.

Once again, they wouldn't disappoint me. Right on schedule, the first bugle of the evening (more like a strange yodel) broke the silence. It was the Screamer telling his harem it was time to get up and go play in the wallow.

Waiting impatiently to see the development of this year's antler growth, I wondered just how big would the Screamer be now? Would he be 380 inches? 390? Bigger? I didn't know and I didn't care. I just knew he was going to be huge and couldn't wait to see him. I felt the excitement elevating because the game was on and he was heading my way!

Each powerful bugle sent chills through me as the cows started to materialize from back in the timber. They disappeared for a moment as they came up the hill to the wallow. I stopped trying to see the bull at this point and settled back into my blind as it was time to get focused on the water hole. One cow after another popped up in front of me, so close I couldn't move! They took turns getting cool drinks of water as the last cow finally past.

The Screamer was bringing up the rear. His bugles became extremely loud, the loudest I've ever heard, as he was also very close now.

With an arrow on the string, I was ready to draw back. The bull, barely below the crest of the hill, bugled again at full volume. Now I was at full draw and about to take the bull elk of a lifetime at just 15 yards!

Like the eighteen cows that passed before him, now it was his turn. The immense bodied bull popped up right in front of me and stood broadside. He let out one final ear splitting bugle! I settled my one and only pin on his heart and said, "...Wait a minute! Where's his horns?" I was mortified! Was this an illusion? A bad dream? No...more like a "Nightmare in Angle Fire!" He had only deformed stumps on top of his head! "What in the....where did his...what happened to..." I said. Then, oblivious to my presence just yards away, he dove into the wallow as I let down my draw.

Wide-eyed and stupefied, I sat right there in my blind for fifteen minutes, watching him roll in the wallow, thrashing the water to a froth, having the time of his life, screaming away...*right in front of me!* I could have shot him at least twenty times! It seems the *Phenomenon* has gotten me yet again, this time in a very cruel manner.

Now, thirty disappointing minutes have gone by. I watched the elk slowly move off into the distance. Daylight was waining and the bugles were getting softer indicating it was safe to get up and move without spooking anything. I waved a final surrendering good-bye before strolling back to camp empty-handed and brokenhearted to say the least.

When I told the guys back in camp my story, and explained how I had the Screamer dead to rights at point-blank range for thirty minutes and didn't shoot him, they said, "Yea-a-a, sure you did, Dave, how close was he...could'a shot him how many times?" "No, really...*I did!*" I went on to describe how the Screamer must have had some kind of freakish accident during early summer antler growth, or got sick, or who knows what may have happened to his majestic set of antlers. All I knew was, now he looked more like an overgrown antelope! That was exactly what his horns resembled! Huge bases with weird curling main beams that were no more than a foot or so tall. Despite his deformity, his attitude remained the same as he still reigned supreme!

My hope was that the Screamer would survive the winter and live to regrow his majestic set of antlers the following summer. However, I was very disappointed to learn that a hunter with a lack of respect took this great animal's life while knowing the Screamer's incredible antler history. He knew his history because *I told him!* He was a guest in my camp who I took under my wing and lead him to take his first elk on a previous hunt. I was deeply saddened by this proud elk's demise, as the Screamer would agree...he deserved better.

Reflecting back over the last couple of years, I can only scratch my head in bewilderment over the bizarre array of events that occurred during the pursuit of this highly respectable animal. The range of emotions he invoked could warrant professional counseling; at the same time, drive your desire to return to elk country for one more go round. But by far, the strangest emotion of all was a few simple, yet inevitable questions: You see, this big animal really didn't have a proverbial *"bag of tricks"* up his sleeve, did he? No. He wasn't so smart that no one could take him, was he? Apparently, not! He was just **BIG,** and for a number of years...very, very lucky.

So, was I just dealt several bad hands in a row? Was it luck at all, or could it have been something much more than that...maybe a *Higher Power* with a flair for the dramatic and an imaginative sense of humor?

Perhaps something by the name of, "...*Divine Antlervention???*"

"Ponderosa Pine annihilated by lightning...
just ten seconds earlier!"

WHAT BIG EYES YOU HAVE!

*W*ho doesn't love corn? Deer love it, turkeys love it, raccoons, squirrels, ducks, geese, everybody loves corn. I personally like everything from corn on the cob to corn *dogs!* But, if theirs one kind of corn I cannot stand...*its standing corn!*

Where you'll find most serious big buck hunters, you'll find corn. If you're very lucky, the farmers will have already harvested all the corn on your behalf, awaiting your arrival!

This rarely happens for me. As a matter of observation, I think all the farmers in the Midwest get together every year and go over my personal hunting schedule, similarly to how I study the lunar tables to plan my hunt dates, then they harvest accordingly. Somehow, that corn just seems to stay standing the whole time I'm up there. Then, just as I'm leaving, driving down the road heading back to Florida, they fire up the John Deere tractors and start cutting it all down! The more I drive, the more tractors I see in the fields. Some farmers will even sacrifice sleep, staying out all night long with their lights on, trying to catch up on all the back work they missed while I was there hunting!

The fall of 2006 was no exception. After reaching my midway point, (my much anticipated annual visit with dear friends in Nashville, Tennessee) it was time to weave through the chaotic maze of infinite road options and walls of unyielding brake lights. Stop and go, I adjust the volume on the stereo. Stop again, only to be reminded how unnatural and out of place this all seems to me. Eager to break through the confines of modern evolution, I couldn't wait to see some standing corn for once!

Driving north on Highway 57, it was no oddity to see some of the corn already harvested. It was just far enough south for the climate to produce the correct residual moisture content per bushel (or lack there of) to give the farmers the green light to let the combines do their annual job.

Making my way up through Kentucky, Southern Illinois, and then Northern Illinois with high hopes of continued cutting, old frustrations began to set in as I noticed the corn still standing straight up for some strange reason. Wisconsin, the same thing. Then it dawned on me. I almost forgot...I was on my annual deer hunting trip!

My first greetings to my farmer friends were the normal, "Hellos" and other cordial questions like, "How have you been? How's the family? ...Planning on gettin' that ol' corn out any time soon?"

Most hunters understand my concern, or should I say, *grievance* about the standing corn. In case you don't, I'll briefly elaborate. In a nutshell, the deer love to hide out in it. They never leave, except maybe at night to get a drink of water after all the hunters are out of the woods. When its standing, they live in it. Why would they go anywhere else? It's like living in a grocery store. So, while we're in the woods hunting them, they're in the cornfields living the life, safe and secure! Just stand by one of these field edge around 4:00 in the afternoon, and you can hear them in there having a big time! "Crunch-crunch, grunt-grunt!" You won't see too many deer in the actual woods.

The first three days of my hunt started out just as I described, but that was okay. I still needed to fill a doe tag in order to receive a buck tag. In this particular hunting unit, you had to shoot a doe first, before you could hunt one with horns. So, I was just out trying to,*"Earn a Buck"*

I opted to sit in a portable ground blind on the edge of an alfalfa field that was scattered with hay bales. It looked very natural, and my landowner friend assured me there were a few does coming out to feed there every afternoon. I'd have no problem filling my doe tag in a hurry.

We got the blind all set up and my friend patted me on the back before leaving and said, "Good luck!" I replied, "Thanks a lot, buddy!" I was happy to be doe hunting. I couldn't wait to get that delicious meat in the freezer. It's my favorite! Then on with the serious business of buck hunting as planned.

It was a quiet afternoon in the blind until thousands upon thousands of Redwing Blackbirds appeared all around me. They were in fall migration mode. Flock after flock would land, take off, and land again. It sounded like a bird chirping convention in full swing! I watched at only inches from my face, as they foraged on seeds or alfalfa or bugs...or whatever they eat. I thought, "Wow, this blind really works great!" Now, if only the does would show up.

It got real quiet again as the noisy birds moved on in a southerly direction. Almost an eerie quiet now, when I heard the unmistakable sounds of dainty footsteps in the crunchy woods. I got ready and nocked an arrow. I grabbed my binoculars to get an early look the does while they were still in the woods. Then one stepped out into the field, off to my right. Swinging the glasses around to get a better look at her, I noticed something unusual...*she had horns!* Holy cow...did she ever! This doe was no doe at all. It was a gigantic 160-inch class 8-point buck! *The buck of my dreams!* Maybe the most beautiful deer I've ever seen; perfection on hooves! If anybody knows me, you would know I've always wanted to get a *monster* 8-point, and this was the one. A true 160-inch class 8-point looks as good as a 190-inch class 10-point any day in my opinion. His rack was very tall, very wide, extra heavy, and heading in my general direction. Only one problem- I only had a doe tag...*no buck tag yet!*

I sat in my blind, anxious as you could ever imagine, wondering how close would this deer come to this fake bale of hay I was sitting in? Watching him through my binoculars as he gorged himself on the alfalfa, I noticed he wasn't bothered by a thing. It was hard to take my eyes off him. He was absolutely **HUGE!**

At about fifty yards, he veered to the left, which is where I was set up, and continued closing the distance in my direction. Chewing away, step by step, he moved to within 25 yards of my blind. I thought, "Cake shot...*if only I had a buck tag!*" However, he wasn't done with his job of completely infuriating me just yet, as he got within 10 yards...yes, *10 yards* from my blind! I could have spit on him...*but I'm not like that!*

Then, he took a couple laps around my blind then stopped directly in front of my main shooting window, looked right in at me, (squinting to confirm the "fine print" on my unfilled doe tag) then went back to feeding.

Unconcerned, he casually swaggered to the other end of the field, and back into the woods and out of sight he went.

I was in udder disbelief as the dairy farmers say up there, and to add a little salt to the wound, my friend watched the whole thing with binoculars from his tractor in the field across the road! He said, (and I quote) "Well, this proves you're not a poacher!" I attempted to chuckle, but the expression on my face said it all, "...I cannot believe that *that* just happened! Why me?"

This buck was so impressive that my farmer friend himself decided to sit in that blind the next day. That was good because I wouldn't have survived a replay, had it occurred. I eventually shook it off and managed to get a doe, and graduated to hunting bucks. After that, I went back and sat in the same ground blind in the same place one more time hoping the big massive 8-point would do a repeat performance...*but, all I saw were does!*

The next day, I went to one of my favorite places up on the hill and sat in my best observation stand, but didn't see much there either. Again, a few more does, maybe a "chipper" buck here and there, but no bruisers. I did hear a bunch of deer out in the corn though!

Confusion set in and I decided to get off the hill and try my luck in the creek bottom the next morning. I felt good about my choice to move, thinking, "Maybe this will be the key!"

It was a beautiful creek about five feet wide, winding around like the shape of a big snake, and carried three feet of flowing water at its deepest point. Some trees were big enough to put a treestand in, but not exactly where I wanted to be. Compromising, I picked what I thought was a good enough tree in a fairly open area with tall grass all around it. This tree seemed to be in the right place- not far away on either end of the creek bottom was standing corn. I couldn't wait for morning to come.

Anticipating a change of luck, I wanted to get into my stand very early as not to disturb any of the deer milling around the area. The stars were still out while I tried to get comfortable and figure out the best position to stay warm and go back to sleep for a while. Now, I would just have to wait for grey light.

I thought I woke myself up by "sawing lumber," when I realized it was a buck grunting and coming through the standing corn. *I was awake now!* He was announcing his presence by thrashing each cornstalk with his antlers as he removed one ear at a time. Then, as he got closer, I could tell he was crushing several rows of corn simultaneously as he walked. This had to be a big buck I thought, but it was still too dark to see.

The buck exited the cornfield and was only forty yards away in the woods, following the edge of the creek, soon to come right under my treestand. Holding the binoculars up in the general direction of the sound, I could see only a dark figure. As he continued toward my ambush site, the massive rack revealed itself, just as my eyes decided to water up! He looked to be some kind of huge non-typical buck, like the type they have in major hunting supply stores! The problem was, it was still too dark to see him without the binoculars.

He slowed down his pace, and began eating grass. It sounded like a horse feeding in a pasture as he pulled up multiple blades of thick, wild grass, one mouthful at a time. Closer and closer he moved, as I strained my teary eyes to see him. My arrow was on the string, and the giant non-typical was now right under my treestand!

I was beside myself as I still didn't have enough light to see the deer clearly. Only a dark, grainy blob fading in and out. There was nothing I could do. I couldn't shoot yet- it was just too dark. My eyes were really *"teary"* now!

This colossal buck hung around for ever it seemed, maybe longer. I think he ate *all* the grass around the tree I was in. The sound was pure torture.

"Baby Button Buck"

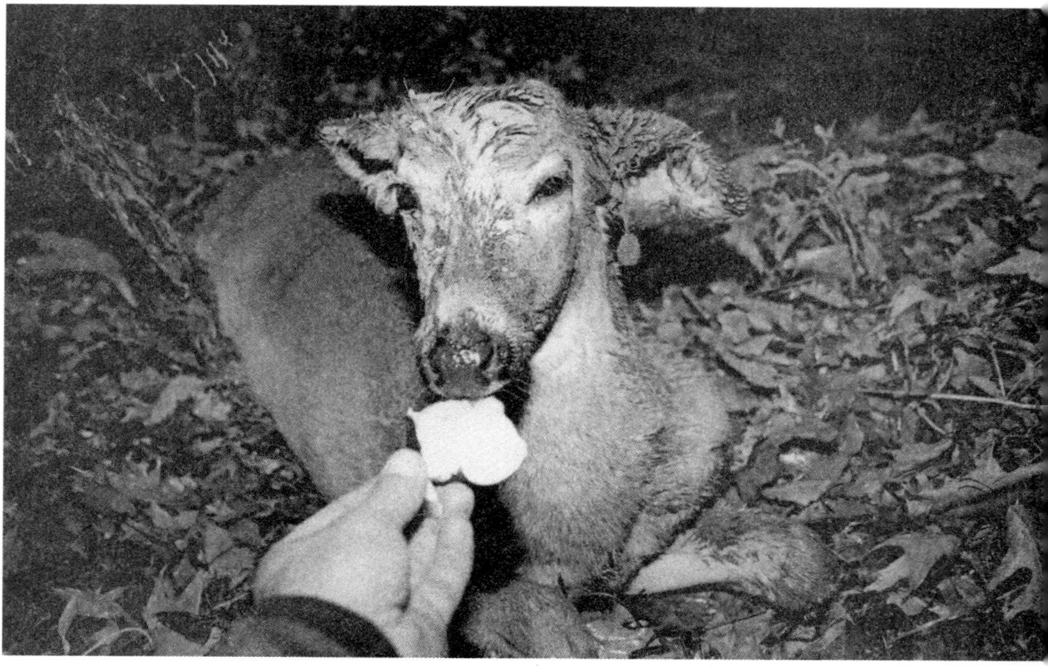

With the buck finally out of bow range, it was now *light enough to shoot!* He was a true non-typical behemoth with more points than I could count. I had to listen to him grunt all the way to the next cornfield to bed down for the day. And yes, I tried everything I could think of to get him back into bow range. I grunted, estrous bleated, (more like estrous *pleaded*), I rattled, snort wheezed...you name it, I tried it! Crying didn't work at all! I even reminded the Big Buck Gods about the baby button buck whose life I saved the year before when he got his two back legs caught in a barbed wire fence and I freed him from the hungry coyotes! He was exasperated...the poor thing! I gave him my last water, an apple, **"Saved his life!"** I reiterated. They said, *"Sorry...that was in Illinois!"*

Back up on the hill I went, that afternoon. I didn't want to go to my favorite stand just yet, which was just inside the woods on the outside corner of a big standing cornfield. So, further back in the timber I went. There's a ridge at the top of a big hill which bucks love to cruise when the rut gets going. That's when they aren't in the corn...cruising! I set a stand that I would return to in the morning.

The first early hour's activity produced a few doe sightings and a small buck. Then, something caught my eye. It was a buck. With one look through the binoculars, I knew he was a shooter! Very slowly, he eased along the top of the ridge in my direction. As I watched him, I noticed how much his rack continued to grow, the closer he came. Then a drop tine came into view. I love drop tines! It's not often you get to see this feature on a deer, especially when he's heading toward you instead of away. I could see one drop tine on his left side but not on his right. However, he was getting too close now to gawk at anymore and I needed to get ready to shoot. Still on course, it was time to focus and make the shot. I drew back, picked an opening and waited. The buck was now walking broadside at 25 yards, about to hit the opening. I grunted and stopped him. I put my one and only pin right on him, carefully studied the shot, and smoothly let the lengthy projectile fly!

Then faster than a speeding arrow, a branch grew out from the side of a cedar tree and deflected my shot to the ground...just about two feet before it would have center punched him in the vitals! The buck ran off simply startled, never to be seen again.

The next day I should have bought a lottery ticket because for no known reason, they started cutting the corn. Of course they would save my area for last. Even though my hunt was almost over, I held on to what little optimism remained as I still had one more day to hunt.

I sat patiently the following morning after they finished harvesting near my #1 stand, because I knew the deer would have to go around the cut fields this time to travel safely back to their bedding cover. My outside corner has become an inside corner, and would be very interesting now!

Early morning, the deer were pouring through the woods past my stand as I was the one giggling now. One after another I counted. I was amazed at how many deer were walking through the woods. A number of decent bucks came by, scent checking the earlier does, but where's my monster buck, I wondered?

I sat and sat, then...Snap! Crunch!...there he was! Quartering down the hill towards me, I could tell he was the one I've been holding out for! (Actually, I think I would have shot two or three different bucks over the last few days, if I remember right...but that didn't matter now!)

Here he came just like I planned, heading right for the corner of the woods I was counting on. Moving steadily forward, he lowered his nose, then slowed down, trying to catch a whiff of the recent does.

He was a big bodied bruiser with a tremendous rack. I was very impressed with this deer. I counted ten or eleven points on his mainframe, somewhere around the mid to upper 170's, and noticed some extra *stuff* on his rack, to boot. He hit the doe trail and hit the brakes. Nose still to the ground, he stood processing the information at only 30 yards, well within shooting range. The trail would come right past my stand at 20 yards, so I wanted to wait for a closer shot. He stepped forward and I drew back.

Suddenly, he turned off the main trail for no apparent reason, and continued walking slowly...right for the tree I was sitting in! I followed him with my one and only sight pin right on him. I wanted him to turn broadside, but he wouldn't do it. He was facing me and still coming closer and closer. Then, at only five yards from my tree, he stopped. He slowly raised his head up and looked me right in the eyes with a surrendering expression as if he knew I was there all along! His rack swept back as I contemplated the angle. I knew I could kill him right then and there, just like that. But, he kept staring at me...almost as if to say, "*Gulp*...this is the end, isn't it?" I stared back, right into those big brown glistening eyes. Then the most peculiar feeling came over me. He reminded me of my beloved black lab who was now in his later years...*I just wanted to pet him!* "What's going on here? *This* has never happened before!"

Time seemed frozen in place. Still drawn back and feeling more sentimental and confused by the moment, I said to the buck, "You better *GO* if you're *GOING*," ...and so he did just that.

I let down my draw as the buck trotted out to about 30 yards, happily wagging his tail, and stopped. He looked back with an expression of deep gratitude and relief, as if to say, "Thank you friend, the Big Buck Gods will reward you for this one day!" I could almost swear he winked at me once, then went on his way. I just shook my head in an attempt to clear the fog in my disorganized brain. *"Whoa...what in the world just happened...?"*

I had to ponder for a moment. In fact-- I pondered for a thousand miles all the way back to Florida because my hunt was officially over.

While driving home with my arm around my Black Lab's neck, I had to stare off into the woods along the Interstate many times and ask myself, "Wow, did I just go all the way to Wisconsin to let a giant buck walk? Am I getting soft or what?" As my elderly dog glanced back at me with *his* big, brown eyes, I wondered, "Was this the ultimate play on my emotions by the creative spirit of *Divine Antlervention*?" Have they gotten *that* clever? Of course not! Why, that was just a little test! Surely the "Big Buck Gods" will reward me tenfold for that act of kindness someday, right? Of course they will, ...of course! Just like they did with the little button buck...*back in Illinois!*

SOME OF THE BEST HUNTS START THIS WAY!

*I*t was the autumn of 2007. After a long, hot summer working on the "Worlds Most Beautiful Beaches," (Panama City Beach, Florida) it was finally time to hit the road and go see some trees. Not palm trees, but real trees...the kind Bill Jordan likes!

With the truck strategically packed down with everything from duffel bags to my favorite phesant gun, one high-pitched, two-finger whistle... and my hyper-excited black lab and I, *"loaded up!"* I waved goodbye to the Gulf of Mexico and exhaled a much needed sigh of relief. Adjusting the seat back a little further, I popped in my favorite *Rascal Flatts* CD and hit the cruise control button. "Gator" rested his head faithfully on my lap as I pointed the compass north.

Gator always seemed to know when we were heading out of town to hunt. He got that look of anticipation in his eye when he saw me trying to quietly sneak the 28 gauge pheasant gun past him and into the back seat of the truck. Then the tail would gain incredible speed, much like it did when we pulled into a Dairy Queen!

Each time we stopped for gas, I noticed how the temperature had dropped a little, indicating we were much further north than where we started. Once again, I had not remembered to put a jacket in the front seat of the truck when we left Florida. Eventually, we saw the first flock of Canadian geese flying in the opposite direction than we were heading and wondered why one side of the V-formation was always longer than the other. Come to find out, the scientific aerodynamic reasoning for this is that there's more geese on that side!

During the course of twenty-four hours, I watched the deciduous trees go from green, to yellow, to orange and red, then finally brown. Thats the color I preferred for hunting. Upon arrival, most of the leaves were already on the ground, indicating I had missed Mother Nature's pre-arranged autumn windstorms. However, the corn was still standing in most places, as one might expect!

The first order of business was to drive the back roads looking for a pheasant or two for Gator to flush. We didn't need to shoot it, he just needed to smell a live, wild bird to advance the senses to let him know we've reached our hunting destination. The poor thing, he'd been stuck in the front seat of a pickup truck for two days with a year-old dried up wing. It was the greatest thrill for me to watch his tail twitch spastically out of control when he got really "bird-y!" Not like it did at home with a frozen version, as this was not a fire drill. This was a real live, warm-scented bird trying to escape his incredibly talented nose.

After refreshing the canine's innate purpose in life, riding in the truck with his head out the window seemed to suffice for the time being, while I scanned the field edges lined with trees, looking for buck rubs that were recognizable from the road. When looking for a good place to start my hunt, this was always simple math to me.

Glassing a familiar hillside brought back memories from a few years ago, when I was lucky enough to put my tag on a 17-point Boone & Crockett buck. I had mouth-called him in with a sultry, seductive estrous bleat to within three yards of my treestand and put an arrow through the main boiler. I say *"lucky"* because it was my first Wisconsin buck on my first Wisconsin hunt. From that point on, *it was all downhill!*

I knew the area where he had lived held some good bucks based on sign from my last visit. It didn't surprise me to see a couple good two and a half and three and a half-year old eight and ten-pointers on my first evening out. The buck I wanted was not going to be in that age group, though. I was after a *Super-Buck!* That potential usually required at least a couple more years growth. I knew the big ones were there and I had plenty of time to try to make it happen.

On the third afternoon, I saw an exceptionally large ten or eleven-point that had something "extra" going on with his rack. It was a little too late in the day to tell exactly what it was, all I knew was it was "extra!"

Some people referred to this extra antler growth as "trash," but not me. I love it. This is the one exception when I would be happy to take out the trash!

Following up the next morning with a little closer-range observation, I saw the same deer exit the alfalfa field through an area of deadfall timber. I made a mental note of his path and direction. Figuring he might want to use the same corridor for a point of entry into the field that evening, I put him to bed for the day and left the area alone. I wore a sly smerk of confidence back to the truck.

The next day, a late breakfast and a little phesant hunting was in order. Both, the food and the pheasants went down as planned. Then my thoughts of *"The Big One"* took over, and I got my first jolt of nervous excitement. It was time for me to get cleaned up and get back in the woods.

Remembering I still had to set up my treestand, I hurried the pace up a little bit since I hadn't even picked out a tree to sit in. Looking at where the deer disappeared into the cover of the dark forest the morning before, I scanned the terrain for some kind of pinch point or funnel or anything I could call an advantage, and found nothing. I arbitrarily chose an observation tree that would offer an up-close and personal look into the deers' world, with hopes of homing in on the exact tree to set up in the next time around.

The afternoon breeze became quite chilly as the weather channel indicated a cold front was expected to move in the following day. That's always welcome news and I was beginning to feel very good about the hunt.

A few deer filtered down into the field toward the evening, including the original eight and ten-pointers I saw the other day. Then, just before *dark-thirty*, a huge-bodied buck revealed itself from the cover, seventy yards up the hill. I threw the binoculars up to confirm that he was the tall, wide rack stud with the "extra stuff" I was after, and...it was definitely him! Almost out of shooting light, I opted for the trusty grunt call and attempted a little *trash talk* on him. As it turned out, he was much too smart for such conceptual semantics and ignored my impersonation.

Darkness fell upon the evening, but the mercury fell faster. All my high-dollar hunting apparel couldn't stop the shivering, although I wasn't so sure it was all due to the temperature. After all, this was a BIG, big buck!

I decided to pass on the next morning's hunt to let things settle down for a while. I knew this buck would be wary from his experience with past hunting seasons, and some extra finesse would be required.

Midday was the time to make a move and relocate the stand uphill, but not too far as to risk alerting the buck to the fact that he had company in the woods. He was smart enough and needed no further education.

The does and smaller bucks were using the same draw consistently to travel from point A to point B, so I focused most of my attention in that direction. The overzealous scrub bucks were acting as if it were Valentine's Day, but even their best advances were declined by the ladies. A couple of nasally grunts by the young bucks, followed by a desperate chase here and there told me the does were heating up and the larger version of eligible bachelors would soon appear on the circuit.

Suddenly, from further up the hill, I heard a *real* grunt! Down the same draw came my target deer! Zeroing in on him with the binoculars, I identified the extra *stuff* on his rack to be drop tines! But, was this the same drop tine buck from the year before...*now with two drop tines?*

Regardless, I was definitely fired up! He was out of range by fifty yards or more as he walked casually through the bottom of the ravine, checking his messages at each scrape and sniffing for information about the does state of estrous. Instead of enlightening the buck any further with another fake grunt call, I let him slip on by me like I wasn't even there...watching his every move.

Suddenly, pieces of a plan flashed together in my mind. I was sure I had pegged his preferred travel route. I now knew, how I would take this special buck.

I decided I would move my stand in the dark long after all the deer had passed by, then set up for the morning hunt. A bold move, but I managed to quietly accomplish this without disturbing any deer in the process. Before I left the woods, I marked the new stand location with my GPS, knowing this would be the only way to find it in the dark the following morning.

Restaurant options in Spring Green were limited, but I wasn't there for the dining experience. However, a big cheeseburger at *"The Shed"* and a Culvers frozen custard was the perfect ticket to top off the day, and send me to dreamland, content with a hopeful smile.

No sooner did I fall asleep when the alarm went off. *"That was quick,"* I thought, and double-checked the time. It was 4:00 a.m. all right. Maybe I was just worn out from all the extra work from moving the treestand in the woods the night before.

With that in mind, it was time to boot-scoot and boogie. Groggy and bleary-eyed, I stuck my head out the motel door to check if I could see my breath. The answer was definitely, "Yes!" The cold front hit and the temperature outside was subfreezing. I had a long trek through the woods to get up the hill and around the deer that would be out feeding in the field. I knew it would take some extra time, so I scrambled together my belongings and left.

After a thirty minute drive to the place where I would start walking, I jumped out of the truck and looked up at the clear dark sky all lit up with a million lucky stars. "What a sign!" I thought. I put my gloves on, took my bow out of the case and set it outside on the frosted, white grass. On with the jacket next. "Wait a minute, where's my jacket?" Oh yeah, I strapped it to my backpack. "Phewww!" Good thing I remembered to do that! "Wait a minute, where's my backpack?" Don't tell me I.......*I did!* I left my backpack with my jacket, binoculars, and G.P.S. back at the motel! I've never done that before...*ever!* I must have had a brain freeze when I stuck my head out the motel door.

Forever being the optimist, I said to myself, "Not a problem, I can find my treestand in the dark without a G.P.S., and it's really not *that* cold out!" So, off I went, thinking, "...Some of the best hunts start out this way!"

Well, it was a lot colder than I had allowed myself to believe. Unfortunately, the polyester camo sweater with a broken zipper I *did* have on, was not one of my high dollar garments. I only wore it so I wouldn't stink up my *good* jacket, ...*my good, warrrm, down jacket!*

Hiking up the logging road helped with the body temperature, but I knew better than to let myself break a sweat. Remembering to keep a fine balance between generating heat and generating too much heat was crucial.

I found the little trail that I had cleverly marked with a log on the way out of the woods the night before and said, "This'll be easy, a piece of cake." At the end of the trail, I would be within thirty yards of my treestand.

Arriving at that point, I had only one question, **"...*Where is it?*"** I stood wondering, looking all the tree trunks over with a diffused flashlight and not recognizing the one I thought would be so easy to find. Searching all around, I even did what I never do and shined my light up in the trees. "Did somebody steal my treestand, or am I just an idiot?"

Well, I felt like the latter of the two as it was now starting to get light out and the first crunchy footsteps were coming my way fast! I could see the deer would all pass by me within bow range, but for some reason, this caught me completely off guard as I said to myself, "Wake up, dummy...*do something!*" I snapped out of my stupor, backed into some deadfall timber, and nocked an arrow onto the string.

The does were on track to come right past me, but without my binoculars, I couldn't tell if my buck was with them. It was still semi-dark out. Then, the lead doe stopped. She only needed a second look to know something was out of place! "Hmmm...a new fixture in the landscape?" she must have thought to herself. I felt like a lawn ornament...maybe a flamingo, or some other out-of-place thing from my home state of Florida. It didn't matter though, they were off and running, snorting away, which sounded more like snickering to me. Then they were gone.

Ridiculous for me to even try to think positive at this point, I put the arrow back in the quiver where it belonged and headed toward the truck.

I didn't take but about two steps and there was my treestand right in front of me! *"Daah"* was nicest four letter word I could think of. In retrospect, I was quite surprised I was that close to finding it in the first place without my G.P.S., as things sure look a lot different in the dark!

Shivering uncontrollably at the base of the tree, I thought, "If I were only up in that treestand five minutes ago, those does would have gone right past me, and who knows what else, *had they not busted me."*

Then...Snap! I looked downhill toward the field to see a big buck chasing a doe, it was none other than my target buck! I ran up those treesteps, clicked onto my safety harness, and pulled my bow up all in one record-setting motion. I nocked an arrow on to the bowstring and watched as they came closer. Clearly, I could see the drop tines on the Big 10! He had to be over 170 inches, maybe 175! At fifty yards and heading my way, he let out a big, deep, hollow grunt, the kind only truly big bucks are capable of making. He was right on that doe's tail as she got closer and closer to me. I said to myself, "See that? Like I said, some of the best hunts start out this way!" Just then, they veered to the right at the *Y* in the trail. Up the hill and out of sight they went. I said to myself, "See that? I knew I should have gone back to the motel and gone back to bed!"

I sat for a little while longer, maybe twenty minutes until I thought I could no longer stand the shivering. All of a sudden- again, crunching leaves broke the silence. Another buck came from the same field chasing another doe! I said, *"See that?..."* Then I noticed it was the same two deer on the same trail coming toward me again. They must have gone in a big circle. My drop tine buck *surely* came back to tease me some more because I knew they were going to turn right at the *Y* intersection again, just like they did twenty minutes before.

But, this time they didn't. They went straight, which would put them on the trail right in front of me! "Thank you Deer Gods!" was all I had to say about that. "I can't believe it, I'm actually going to get a crack at this big guy after all that nonsense!" I drew back my bowstring and picked the perfect shooting lane they were about to enter at only 23 yards. The doe went through the opening first, then the buck. I grunted to stop him...*"Mrruutt!"* My pin was on him as he stood perfectly still, broadside. I studied the shot, took careful aim, and confidently released.

The arrow looked to be right on target, then at the last split-second, it took a nose dive and somehow passed harmlessly underneath the buck's vitals.

The big deer ran off unscathed and continued his romantic pursuit. I immediately looked for the *"culprit branch"* I was sure must have just sprouted! But this time there was none. "What happened?" I wondered. All *that,* and I misjudged the shot? This time, it was simply, *"Arrow-dynamics"* that caused this miss! Hunter error! Either way, especially after the shot, he sure did look a lot like the drop tine buck from the year before...*running free!*

With the most befuddled look on my face, my 2007 Wisconsin deer hunt ended just that way...*befuddled!* So much for my perfect plan! It took days for the facial contortions to dissipate, but my eyes will always remain somewhat crossed with the memory of events that bring us to the end of this story...*I think you already know the moral!*

TIMING IS EVERYTHING

*M*y second whitetail hunt of the year happens in Illinois, immediately following my hunt in Wisconsin. I like to go to Wisconsin first because the rut activity seems to turn on a little earlier up there, most likely due to the cooler weather. If everything goes as planned, I'm leaving Wisconsin on or around the eighth day of November with a racked buck in the back of my truck. That's always a good way to start an Illinois deer hunt...but does it ever go *as planned?*

I've hunted most major big buck counties in Illinois including Pike, Scott, Brown, Fulton, Schuyler, McDonough and a few others. My favorite county is all the ones I've mentioned. They are all great places to hunt and each has ***monster*** potential. Pike county gets the most attention, and I can vouch for it myself since my biggest archery buck to date came from that county. Even though he didn't quite hit my goal number of 200 inches, I'm just as proud as if he had! However, I've seen a number of larger deer in almost all the other counties mentioned. This is where last years story takes place...in Schuyler County.

Schuyler County, just north across the Brown County line, doesn't get the same attention as Pike and some of the other famous Illinois counties for some odd reason. It could be that many out of state hunters have had such good luck in Pike County, that more and more hunters want to go there. The monster bucks just keep "racking up" year after year. A testament to good management!

Divine Antlervention

Dave Panetti

A good friend of mine gave me permission to bowhunt his family farm, which I am forever grateful to be considered that close of a friend. Usually, when hunting land that you don't own yourself, there's a few rules included in the deal. Rule #1 is: Always obey the landowners rules. Whatever the landowners rules are, *you do it!* Even if you don't agree with everything, you do it anyway. This statement will prove to have a profound affect on this hunt, and on with the story we go.

November the 12th was a perfect day to be in the Illinois woods in for an autumn afternoon bowhunt. There was a chill was in the air that was conducive to early deer movement and early jitters as well. The excitement level went up while the outside temperature went down.

I was in a tree stand in a deep "hollar," as they say up there. (I call these ravines.) A very good looking hollar where three separate hills connect at their bases, causing them all to meet at a winding creek bottom. A maze of deer trails criss crossed everywhere, looking more like cattle trails in some places. Just above, the fresh cut cornfeilds were like powerful deer magnets.

Big buck rubs were scattered everywhere and I knew I was in for some action this particular day when a beautiful 10-point buck walked through the area in the middle of the afternoon while I was in the process of hanging my treestand. I should have expected that! It wasn't the first time I've had to become a "treehugger," clinging to one side to let a deer pass. At 140 inches, he was no shooter buck on this day's hunt, but happy to see, nonetheless. I was after something much larger; the one to beat all other bucks!

The owner of the property was hunting on another hill across the cornfield from me, about a quarter of a mile away. With only one rule to abide by, he asked that I only hunt the property when he was there and hunting as well. No big deal, except he didn't like to get up in the morning when most serious hunters did, and he liked to leave the woods in the evening earlier than what I consider normal.

This particular afternoon was no exception. In fact, he wanted to leave the woods even earlier today to go to an Elks Club meeting! I had a *"meeting"* planned myself that afternoon with a big buck and didn't want to miss it, but had to agree to the plan, as much as it flustered me to do so. Like I said, "Always abide by the landowners rules."

Five o'clock was the time he choose to meet back at the truck so we wouldn't be late for the important social event. I was dreading the thought of leaving the woods that early because I knew the does would be on the move at this time, heading for the smorgasbord just uphill from my stand.

The early afternoon had passed with plenty of young buck sightings and a few does. The 140 inch class 10-point that walked by earlier seemed to rule the creek bottom as he put on a two hour show for me and the does, chasing all the younger bucks out of his area.

All the does had eventually passed by on the way to get groceries, and now, with it getting closer to prime time, it was also getting closer to *"out-of-time"* for me. My watch kept inching forward to the dreaded 5:00 mark. I still had to hike a half mile back to the truck, but I squeezed every last second out of my allotted time slot I could. After a lengthy battle with my conscience, guilt finally caved-in to this mental tug-of-war. While grinding my teeth, I mumbled a few "rasum-frasum" type adjectives under my breath, then proceeded to wrap it up.

One item at a time, I quietly slipped all the cleverly marketed buck hunting gadgets into my hanging backpack. With one last look around, I clipped my bow and backpack to my hoist rope and slowly lowered both down to the forest floor. At the precise moment the bow touched the ground, the unmistakable snap of a medium sized twig sent a high-voltage shockwave through the entire length of my body!

From the cornfield above at just fifty yards uphill, a buck was coming down the trail in front of me at a very brisk and determined pace. I spontaneously brought my binoculars up to get an accurate assessment of him, although my gut somehow knew it was probably a monster. *It was!* Not just any monster, it was the *ultimate monster!"* Perhaps bigger than any Pike County giant I've ever seen!

In a moment of stunned disbelief, then the gravity of the situation sank in! Here was my Illinois buck of a lifetime closing in on me and soon to run right past me and out of my life forever, and I didn't even have my bow in my hand. It was lying on the ground... *fifteen feet away!* Still in shock with the question of what I should do, the answer finally hit me, **"...Something...anything!!!"** Frantically, I took my own advice and quickly pulled up on the tote rope, hand over fist, and reunited with my bow and backpack in record time. I untangled the two items and awkwardly held my pack between my feet on the floor of the tree stand.

All I could see was an enormous nontypical 200-inch rack with great mass and points going every which direction, well within my shooting range. I didn't even have an arrow nocked yet! Still coming at just seven yards facing me and about to give me a four yard broadside shot, I finally managed to get the arrow *out of the quiver!* Fumbling to connect the two most important components, arrow and string, the buck now passed the base of my tree at three yards and is quartering away! I had to stop him even though I wasn't drawn back on him yet. I grunted as I was making sure the arrow was in the correct place under the nockpoint. Unaware of the fact that I was right above him, he stopped right on cue! I drew back and quickly put my one and only pin where it needed to be, and just a *split microsecond* before I could release the arrow, he took off running again! My upper body semi-collapsed as I somehow managed to hang on to the bowstring.

I regained full draw again as I grunted louder to stop him a second time...but to no avail. He had somewhere else he needed to be, and it wasn't an Elks Club meeting. *"...Whoops!"* That reminded me!

Since I was already packed up, it only took a second or two to slip out of the stand and scurry back to the truck. I was a few minutes late, but I had one glamorous excuse!

So, what really happened back there in the woods? *Bad timing?* Maybe...but I don't think so. You see, any other day, I would never even think of leaving my stand that early, especially in the second week of November in Illinois! Any other day, I would have been at full alert with bow-in-hand when that twig snapped, and "Mr. Monster-Buck" would be over "Mr. Fireplace" right now as we speak!

So, why was it that on that particular day, when I was coaxed out of the woods just a few minutes earlier than usual, did the King of Bucks grace me with his presence at the ***exact*** moment he did? I always say,

"Timing is everything...*or is it?*" Was it timing at all...or was it just dumb luck that kept this rarest of bucks alive and denied this respectful, agreeing hunter a bonafide two-hundred incher? That certainly seems to be the case from my point of view. But, is timing really *everything?* Perhaps it could be, or is it possible this was an elaborate diversion by the phenomenon in question all along?

I have my own theory...but I'm going to let the fellows back at the Elks Club decide this one!

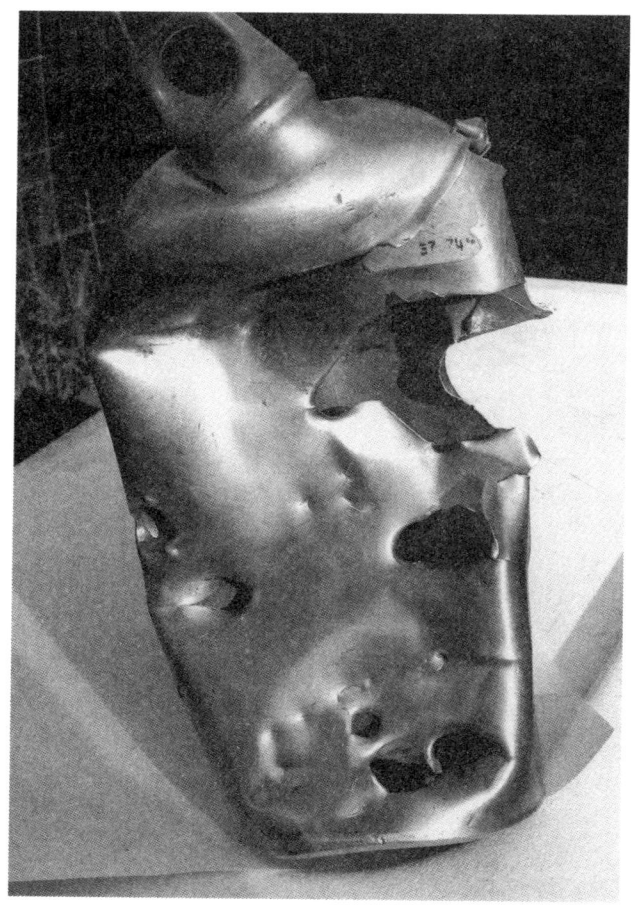

"Destroyed gas can"

ALASKAN DREAM HUNT

*A*fter years of planning and saving, it was finally time to board a plane in San Diego and leave for our Alaskan moose and caribou hunt. My good friend, Chris Lorea and I had every detail worked out and we were on our way. Our dream hunt was really happening!

All went according to plan, until we arrived in the little town of Naknuk on the Alaskan peninsula. The September weather was normal for this time of year...*rain and more rain!* However, wind mixed with rain was a problem for flying. This last civilized town would hold us captive for three days awaiting better weather before we would hop on a float plane to our final destination to begin our hunt.

We were stuck in a small hotel with nothing to do but wait. To pass the time, we went over to the local restaurant, ordered the one and only thing on the menu- Cheeseburgers, as we watched the weather report on TV. We did noticed other planes were flying out, though...

After three days of anxiously awaiting the "green light," our bush pilot said it was time to go! We were flying to Mt. Pulik, which was approximately one hundred miles to the west. On our way there, we flew over a couple of caribou hunting camps in the rugged terrain, and couldn't wait to get to ours.

After a long flight, our plane finally touched down on one of Alaska's most beautiful and serene wilderness lakes we've ever seen! The glassy surface was dotted with rain drops, but the reflection of the mountains in the background was still quite remarkable. Our pontoons gracefully skimmed the water as the engine seemed to *"stall out,"* lowering the plane down onto the lake's surface and converting it into a boat.

Upon reaching the shore, the pilot let us out with all our gear and said he would pick us up at the same location in seven days. We were very excited to be there. Although the weather was dismal at best, the intensity of our excitement kept our spirits high, as we waved good-bye to the pilot.

    The first order of business was to climb to the top of a hill for a better look at the area, and decide where to set up our camp. Not five minutes had passed when Chris said, "Dave, look at the size of that Grizzly Bear coming right towards us!" I thought he was just trying to be funny and I replied, "Chris...don't start with the Grizzly Bear stuff already, we just got here!" Unfortunately, he wasn't joking. Right in front of our eyes was a giant Grizzly Bear heading our way! He was rolling boulders over with one paw while grabbing bugs or rodents or whatever was under there, with the other paw. A quick check on the wind direction and we quickly slipped away, undetected.

    The sight of a giant Grizzly bear toying with huge boulders was one to behold, but we were too close for comfort! After circling downwind for a mile or two, we settled on a good place for a base camp.

    We chose the perfect little grassy meadow in a lower creek bottom that had flowing water. Upon each return from a long day's hunt, we could easily inspect the camp for bears from the hill above.

    Hunting the mixed terrain was tricky. One minute we were slowly trudging through boggy tundra and the next moment we were sliding down a thick willow covered slope, right into an abandoned bear's den with old chewed up bones scattered everywhere!

    By the fourth day, we had a large moose and a caribou down. After packing everything out, we put all the meat in plastic bags and set it in the ice cold creek at least a quarter mile away from our camp. The antlers were set on top of big boulders in the same area.

    Returning to camp the next day following our hunt, we stopped at our usual observation point on top of the hill to inspect our campsite. To our shock and astonishment...*it was gone!* The bears had torn it completely down! We were surprised at how fast they had found it. Not only did they find our camp, they *ate* our camp! These grizzlies ate everything we had. They opened everything that was closed and consumed whatever was inside. They didn't care what it was, they just ate it. On the menu was a spotting scope, tripod, the case it was in, part of our tent, and a one quart can of white gas for cooking. This can was made of super-tough aircraft aluminum, which was full until the bears bit right through it! Maybe they weren't fond of the flavor of white gas because they annihilated the can in disapproval! (See picture on first page of this chapter.) Then they ate **all** of our food, which was hanging high in a tree, leaving us nothing!

Later upon further cautious inspection downstream, we found most of our moose and caribou meat had been eaten as well. At that point, we were sure there was more than one bear at this picnic. Our antlers were also dragged into the brush and chewed on for dessert. (or toothpicks!)

We knew we were in a very bad situation and the bears were probably not far away. Our thoughts flashed back to all the bones we found lying on the ground in the abandoned den just days earlier. Knowing they would soon be back for another meal, we grabbed all we could salvage and packed it out. We headed toward the lake where the floatplane would pick us up in two days.

All hunting was now over. With all our food gone, much of our gear destroyed, and the strong possibility of grizzlies nearby, survival became our only focus. Our dream hunt had become a very *bad* dream! What very little food we had in our backpacks, which was nothing more than picked-over trail mix and stale granola bars, had to hold us over. We could have shot ptarmigans for dinner, or cut up some of the moose steaks that the bears missed, but didn't have any gas to cook them with.

After the bears opened and drained our fuel bottles with their sharp teeth and powerful jaws, it was all but impossible to have a roaring fire in the rain. We managed to start a few smoldering campfires from wet twigs; barely enough to send a smoke signal, much less to cook with or keep us warm and dry. Our gortex jackets weren't much help, as we were completely saturated from the persistent rain. Everything we had was wet as the soggy tundra we were stranded on. The rain never let up and we remained soaked right down to the bone.

Finally it was day seven, the day our bush pilot was scheduled to pick us up. From our new campsite at the lake, we listened patiently for the distant engine rumble as the day came and the day went; only to be let down by the silence of the "unfriendly" skies. No plane showed up at the lake. "Where was he," we wondered?

As night fell upon us we said, "No problem, surely he'll be here in the morning." We both agreed.

After a restless night, we were ready to be picked up. We got excited as a plane noise was finally coming from the distance. We were about to be wisked back to civilization!

The plane went right by without circling. *"What? Where's he going?"* Apparently right past us. "Didn't he see us? This is the right lake, isn't it?" All day we waited for the plane to return for us, but it never happened. Now the thoughts of isolation were making us nervous!

The ninth day, this time...***no plane at all!*** We were becoming very concerned at this point. What could have possibly gone wrong?

Day ten! With bags of rotting and decaying meat now semi-submerged in the chilly lake, we were soaking wet and shivering. We ran out of granola bars, then...a distant plane! "Finally," we said!

He too flew right by us and continued on out of sight! This was crazy! What is going on here? Where was our pilot we hired? Did his plane crash without anyone knowing we were here? Were we in ***real*** trouble now? Big time...because we knew the Grizzly bears would remember us!

That night, Chris and I were wide awake pondering the possibilities of our fate and bargaining with each other over the last few peanuts for the tastier M&M's. With only the green one's left, their color didn't matter any more. Pitch black outside, we were sure every noise around our makeshift tent was the Grizzly bears coming to finish off the rancid meat still in the lake...or would they prefer...***"fresh meat?"***

Daylight on the eleventh morning finally came, and we were still alive. Starvation was the prevailing drive for us now and our only option for survival was to set our compasses toward civilization and start walking. Hopefully, someone would remember us and come looking.

The next thing we saw was a float plane coming in for a landing! It looked like a big "cheeseburger" with wings! We were elated- and furious at the same time. Questioning the pilot, he said, "Sorry, we had bad weather!" We thought, "Well, how were all those other planes flying in that *bad weather?"* At this point we were just thankful he finally showed up!

We loaded our gear and antlers onto the plane, then went to load the rotten meat in the plastic bags. The pilot stopped us and said, "You're not putting that rotten meat on *my* plane!" We told him, "We had to...*it was the law!"* He flatly refused and angrily replied, "**Once again,** that meat isn't going on my airplane and I'm leaving!" He was dead serious! We had no choice. He made us leave the meat behind.

After the one hundred mile flight back to civilization, we stepped from the plane onto the dock in Naknuk. We were greeted by the friendly welcome committee...*the Alaska Department of Fish and Game!* Apparently, someone had called to notify them of the antlers we brought back and lack of meat! *Humm...I wonder who that could have been?*

Needless to say, we were in trouble even though the laws had provisions for each situation we encountered. (1) *The weather:* In the pilots own words, "Kept him from picking us up." It was labeled, "an act of God" in the law book and was out of our control. (2) *The bears:* they attacked our camp and ate most of the meat, and were "protected" as written in the law books, another legal reason not to have adequate meat, and (3) *the pilot* refused to take what meat we did have, on his plane.

Come to find out, the pilot's wife worked for the Alaska Dept. of Fish & Game, and rumor has it any person who reported a violation got "rewarded" with a commission!

We were supposed to be protected by the law, but it didn't happen that way. We even offered to pay for another flight for the Fish & Game officers to see for themselves the boned out carcasses and floating meat in the lake. They declined our generosity, confiscated the antlers, and awarded us with fines for our honesty!

We were very surprised to see how many other hunters in that little town were fined for other frivolous matters. All I know is we were two very brokenhearted young men who weren't sure of what had just happened. At this point, we were just happy to be on our way back to *America*, and that's the way it went for us and our "Alaskan dream hunt." Maybe Sara Palin could help us out with this one!

To this day we still question the whole ordeal. The chewed up gas can and *surviving to tell the story* are the only souvenirs we have to show for this trip!

But, were these really "Acts of God?" or, "Acts of Nature?" Or, were they "Acts of a Spirit" of some other conspicuous arrangement? Either case, I have my opinion...and it will take an "Act of Congress" to change my mind!

THIRD TIMES' A CHARM (or is it?)

Mention the state of Wisconsin to any deer hunter and suddenly that person is like a lovestruck Whitetail buck in mid-October who just got his first whiff of an early estrous doe...*you have his full attention!* And, for good reason. Wisconsin is one of the prettiest places on the face of the earth and it has some of the biggest bucks ever to grace the pages of many a whitetail magazine. Some of them, I know from past hunts are still out there, as you will learn later in this story.

I look forward to bowhunting Wisconsin every year for a number of reasons. Great friends, the best cheese in the world, and as mentioned earlier, plenty of large bodied, cornfed deer. But- there's always one big buck that seems to haunt me each and every year. Sometimes for several years in a row, as the 2008 season was no exception. Yes, this hunt did have a surprise ending...a very **big** surprise!

I usually try to arrive in Wisconsin a couple days earlier than I intend to hunt, so I can scout for big bucks from a distance, using a good pair of binoculars. I look for big rubs in a dominant buck's primary area this way, with very little intrusion or disturbance. This is very relaxing to me, and after a twenty hour drive up from Florida, it gives my senses time to adjust. Once I locate the most promising sign, I sit back and observe, or just *watch the show.* I generally look for doe travel patterns and bedding areas at this time of the year. But, if a particularly large buck seems to have a weakness in his travel routine heading towards one of his scrapes or rubs- such as a wrong turn with the right wind, its time to move in for a closer check on the situation. Maybe even, *checkmate!*

With binoculars, I watched an extremely wide ten point buck move in to freshen one such scrape area, and decided he was big enough to go after. I watched him do his macho buck routine for the does, then he moved on to the bedding area a couple hundred yards away. That's when I snuck in, set up my stand, and snuck out literally undetected awaiting the evening hunt.

That afternoon, after climbing back into my lock-on tree stand, I had a good feeling about this set up. I was about 18 feet up, which is a little high, but it was to make sure that the wind was less of an issue in this particular stand.

Shortly after settling in, as the sunlight was fading to an Autumn amber glow, the first audible footsteps of the afternoon instantly caught my attention. The big bodied, wide rack 10-point was doing his very best to soften his approach as he got closer and closer to his first ground scrape, 30 yards away. I noticed he had a unique feature on his left antler. It was a hole in the end of the main beam that had to be the work of summer flies, or physical damage during early antler growth. It would become his official identification mark. I thought this would be the closest thing I'd ever see to the famous "Hole in the horn" buck and I wanted to take this one.

He put on a show for me, freshening up his scrape line, raking trees, followed by deep guttural grunts. Then he blew a couple snort wheezes which you don't get to hear too often in the deer woods. My eyes were transfixed on him as he moved closer toward me, heading for his primary scrape.

At 18 yards, I quietly drew back an arrow, waiting for him to make that one last fatal step into the opening. A chip-shot from my compound bow would undoubtably do its job, but then suddenly- he froze like an ice sculpture. Moving only my eyes, I saw three does to my left at no less than 15 yards staring straight up at me! I never saw them coming. I was too engrossed in the bucks rituals. One moment I think I have this bowhunting stuff wired, and the next moment, I'm a rookie!

The lead doe voiced an alarm snort so loud, it sounded like a tire blowing out on the freeway. It almost scared me out of my tree! I'm sure it was just to rub in how close they got to me without being detected, and to tell the hole in the horn buck he'd better come along too if he knows what's good for him! So, without a second thought, they all scattered off in different directions, waving goodbye with their white tails and snorting away into the distance.

I waited until after dark to leave the woods, as if any deer would come within a mile or two of such a snortfest. Then, tucked my tail and headed back to the truck. I described this buck to my brother Tony and told him this was the one I wanted to take. But, would I ever see this buck again? Only if I did what he did...*move to a new area!*

Two days later, hunting from my favorite observation stand called "The Saddle," I glassed into the afternoon hours. There wasn't a critter stirring, until suddenly, a large body deer caught my eye from a couple of hills over. I put the Leica 8x42 binoculars on him and the first thing I noticed was a big, wide rack with a hole in the left main beam. (Amazing what you see with a good pair of binoculars!) I immediately had to come up with a plan to get this buck to change directions and come within shooting distance. *I had no plan!* I defaulted to my old standby, and blew on my trusty grunt call. I let a couple notes fly with no response. Then I adjusted the call to a baritone level and turned the volume up a notch, and again *nothing!* He was getting ready to disappear over the last hill when a plan finally popped into my scrambling mind. I remembered, he liked to "snort wheeze" at other deer, so I wondered how he'd like it if I "snort wheezed" at him? Well, he didn't! He hung an immediate left, turned his ears back, lowered his head, and came right at me.

Closing the distance, he disappeared behind the last hill between us. I listened for a moment and heard nothing. Thinking that when he emerged, he would be right in front of me at 20 yards, (since I knew how the deer trails curved around this hill) I drew back my bow and waited. Unfortunately, he knew more trails than I did and had a different idea. Instead, he came straight over the hill above me and to my left, inquisitively looking down at me from twenty yards to the North. The problem was I was drawn back at a 90 degree angle to the East! My compass was off, and again...*so was the buck!*

I returned to the truck that evening to meet Tony. I walked slowly to acquire a little time to conjure up a good excuse as to why the same buck that defeated me at this game of wits just two days earlier, beat me again today and was still running free. The only de-humiliating excuse I could come up with was that *he* was a lot smarter than *I* was...and that was that!

It was two crisp, chilly autumn days later, November the sixth. Going back to the fundamentals was in order. I returned to an area at the base of two adjoining hills which was covered up in huge fresh rubs and a couple of four and five foot wide primary scrapes. The kind that only big bucks like the one I was after have the attitude and horsepower to make!

While on stand for the afternoon hunt, I knew this could possibly be the last day of our hunt. Not because the season was about to end, or my facetious overconfidence in choosing perfect stand locations, (only the deer know that and they aren't talking!) but because my Father back in Pennsylvania was fighting the final battle of his life. A combination of multiple sclerosis and old age was closing in on him quickly. We knew it was just a matter of time until *that* phone call would come.

Around 4:00 that afternoon, a small two and a half year old 8-point buck would break the silence with an immature, squeally sounding grunt. Then a full speed chase after the hot doe that he thought was mutually enamored, was on. Leaves were flying up in the air behind them as she tried to put some distance between herself and the hopeful romantic! On a well-worn trail, straight down the hill past my stand they went, as I somehow had the presence of mind to check the distance with my laser range finder as they sped by. Thirty-seven yards was the magic number to store in the back of my mind, just in case...and before I could put my range finder back into the side pocket of my jacket, here came another deer on the same hill, coming down the same trail at the same speed. I switched out my range finder for the trusty 8x42 binoculars. It was a big wide racked 10-point buck with an unmistakable hole in the left main beam. You got it, the same buck that humbled me twice before is now going for number three!

On the trail, I knew the one opening for a shot was coming up quick. So, I drew back my bow, put the pin there, and waited for the precise moment to let out a loud, oral grunt call to stop the deer. He slammed on the breaks and slid right into the thirty-seven yard opening as if I had planned it that way! The arrow flew true. I watched as the heart shot buck did an immediate 180 degree U-turn and headed back up the hill.

No more than 5 seconds later and fifty yards away, the 24-inch wide hole in the horn buck was finally down...I couldn't believe it! Wow, was this game finally over? A resounding *"Checkmate!"* reverberated.

I glassed the deer from my tree stand and was elated to see the bucks rack sticking up two feet off the ground. What a sight! As I tried to rough score the buck from the stand, I guessed him to be easily in the upper Pope & Young range. I was tickled to say the least!

Since it was only 4:15 p.m., I fired up the cell phone to make a couple of early celebratory phone calls. I called my buddy Bob Fromme, owner of Performance Archery in San Diego.

While living in California for over twelve years, Bob and I did everything together as great friends do. We met, working as laborers for a construction company back in the day, sweeping floors and carrying lumber to the carpenters. Within the first thirty-seconds of meeting each other, we very quickly discovered we had bowhunting in common. On the job, we would always sweep the sawdust and debris to the same central location so we could talk about hunting. Then we learned a unique way to help each other carry lumber around the job site to wherever it was needed: Bob would get one end of an eight foot 2x4 and I would get the other end so we could finish our conversation. This got us nearly fired on more than one occasion!

On the phone, I whispered a few details of the hunt, as not to disturb the woods any more than I already had, got my verbal pat on the back and then hung up the phone.

Returning to the binoculars to gawk a little more at my trophy, I thought this was too good to be true. The buck that got away twice before was now going to get a ride in my truck back to Florida with me.

As they say, "Third time's a charm...*or is it?*" When all of a sudden, he had one more *trick* up his sleeve!

As I had my buck centered in the field of view of my binoculars, a large brown figure entered the scene. I nearly fell out of the treestand when I realized what I was looking at! My celebration was quickly tempered as a behemoth typical buck, the likes of which you only see once in a lifetime, walked right up to my buck! I lowered the binoculars from my face, than physically put my lower mandible back in place. My eyes bulged forward and blinked twice to confirm the reality of the vision in front of me.

With his head lowered, ears laid back, and entire body hair bristled up, this 190 inch-*plus* megabuck was about to inflict some serious damage to this post mortal intruder I had just shot!

The three hundred pound angry beast circled around as if to size up his unyielding adversary, then kicked leaves and dirt in his face, but couldn't get a response. With the big buck still circling, and a little bewildered, I felt a psychosomatic reaction of dirt and leaves being kicked in *my* face also, as if to say, "...You dummy, those are *my* scrapes and rubs you were hunting over!" Hence a final insult!

The world class typical dark horned monster sauntered back into his hiding place. Then all was quiet...*very quiet!* I sat dumbfounded until darkness overcame the forest. Many thoughts went through my humbled mind while I waited to catch a glimpse of my brother's distant flashlight indicating it was time to go intercept him on the ridge. I couldn't wait to exchange the stories of the day. I thought he would have to have some kind of fabricated fairy tale to beat my real life narrative!

After relating my incredible story to my brother, we had one big job ahead of us. We still had to get my buck out of the woods. With a freshly broken leg, which had happened to me just a few months before the season, Tony suddenly realized why I was more than happy to invite him to go with me on this trip to my secret honey hole. Someone had to drag my deer out of the woods! And, have you ever noticed, big deer never get dragged downhill?

After checking my buck in at the local watering hole, better know as the "I-Diehl Tap" in the small town of Plain, Wisconsin, a mini celebration ensued to honor this deer with a couple ice cold mugs of Spotted Cow microbrew. After meeting half the local population, a few pictures of the buck were taken by the lovely bartender-*ess* to adorn their walls.

We then headed back home to the Spring Green Motel to show everyone my buck. I say, home because owners Tami and Fred Gruber, and kids are very dear friends of mine and treat us like we are true family.

Immediately following the celebration, the comfort of a good mattress and a much needed session of deep sleep was in order! No doubt, a solemn reflection of the weeks incredible events would come first.

As I lay in bed with my fingers interlaced behind my head, I stared straight up at the dark ceiling as flashbacks of the afternoon events replayed over and over in my head. As happy as I was with my "Hole in the horn buck," I couldn't help but wonder, "...Why was it that right *after* I shot this highly elusive deer, the Grandaddy of them all came out of the woodwork to dwarf my accomplishment and haunt me with a vision of what could have been,"...My buck of a lifetime!" Was it to lure me back next year for another round of Nature's ultimate game of chess? Or was it something even more omnipresent...the mischievous, yet very skilled phenomenon known as..."*Divine Antlervention?!*"

THE EARLY WARNING SIGNS

I look back sometimes and have to chuckle at the journey of events that lead me to spending so much time in the woods, as I now do. Growing up in Plainfield, New Jersey was no wilderness by any stretch. As a five-year-old child, we had playgrounds- not hunting grounds, no fields or forests, and we had public swimming pools- not lakes or ponds. The only tracks I could follow were train tracks! This was not considered a rural town by any means, even in those days. There were paved streets and sidewalks, fire hydrants and houses everywhere. For fun, our friends would come over to play hide and seek in the back yard, or we'd go to their house to play in the basement. Other than that, we had school. Kindergarten to be exact!

I thought school was lots of fun because I got to play with other kids. We drew pictures with crayons, (mostly animal pictures for me) and cut them out with scissors. Apparently, my kindergarten teacher didn't consider me her favorite student because my end of the year report card said, (and I quote)"...David is loud, bothers others, and needs help with scissors!" (end quote) Wow! Talk about early imprinting! Well, I wish my teacher could see me now- *I've really improved with those scissors!*

One of the earliest memories I had as a five year old, was when my Father went on the TV game show, *The Price is Right!* That was when the host of the show was Bill Cullen! So, we're going back a few years here, *and he won big!* He didn't win the condo in Florida, (yes, they really did give away a condo in Florida on that episode) but he won a boat, and so many cans of Hilton's Oyster Stew, I think we're still giving it away!

We sold the boat to buy a house in northern New Jersey. Glen Gardner was a rural area with a few housing developments popping up here and there, but mostly, it was fields and forests. We had a big yard surrounded by woods and it was common to look out the window in the morning or at night and see deer...in our own backyard!

My Dad bowhunted occasionally with an old wooden stick-bow and cedar shaft arrows. I still have that old bow and a couple arrows to this day, thanks to my cousin Jeff, who had the foresight to hold on to it for me.

One afternoon, a big 8-point buck was walking through the ragweed field across the dirt road we lived on, towards our property. My brother and sisters were all playing outside when we spotted him, and we ran to tell my Dad so he could shoot him! It was archery season, so he got ready.

The biggest deer we kids have ever seen to this point in our young lives was about to walk within bow range of my Dad and we all got to watch from the kitchen window! Were we so excited, we couldn't stand it! At just 20 yards, my Dad drew back his trusty wooden bow when suddenly for no apparent reason, the buck stopped right next to an apple tree, turned broadside and vomited profusely! He continued this until my Dad withdrew his deadly intentions. Then, the buck turned and walked away with his head held low, seemingly to go recover somewhere in the forest!

My Dad explained that the buck was sick, so he didn't want to shoot him. Well, in retrospect, so am I, because I should have paid better attention to that buck's little stratagem so many years ago! *"Hmm..."*

From age six to age eleven, my older brother Tony, Tim Kinney, (my best friend from the neighborhood) and I were inseparable. On the bus, to and from Lebanon Township Elementary School, our noses were "frozen" to the windows trying to see who could spot the most deer. After school, we couldn't wait to get off the bus and get in the woods. Even at that early age, we could name every deer within a mile of our homes, what they ate, where they ate it, and at what time they would show up to do so!

One day after school, with our homemade bows and arrows, we decided to wait in a big Red Oak tree behind Tim's house for a particular group of does we knew would walk their regular trail at exactly 4:30 in the afternoon, searching for acorns. We looked like three monkeys sitting up there on that big oak branch, giggling away, waiting until they got there.

Right on schedule, there they were! The same three deer, the same time as yesterday, walking the same trail, in the same order. *"Shut up, shut up, here they come,"* we quietly shouted at each other! We were so nervous...we had *doe fever!*

As they approached the predetermined location right under our tree, our plan was to draw back our non-lethal, "fake" bows, count to three and shoot. *"One, two, three!"* Fling, flang, fling! Our blunt arrows corkscrewed in three directions, and at a blazing five feet per second, one arrow actually did harmlessly bump one of the does in the back rump area! All the deer scattered, took off running and snorting as we nearly fell out of the tree laughing! To this day, we still argue who the "lucky" arrow belonged to. I say it was mine, but I'm finally beginning to second guess that long held impression!

After the fifth grade, we moved south to a little quaint beach community named Ocean Gate, New Jersey. I loved living there from sixth grade to my early teens. Some of my best friends to this day still live there. My freshman high school sweetheart Bonnie Moore, and I still talk with each other to this day. She is a renown Psychologist in Houston, Texas and owns her own practice called *Purpose Psychology*. This is no coincidence! I may need to call someday to discuss my deer hunting *purpose* with her! For that matter, my little sister Suzanne is also a Psychologist in Ithaca, New York and owns her own private practice called *Life in Harmony Counseling*. So far my hunting *life* has been anything but, in *harmony!* Either way, its nice to know I'm surrounded by so much support!

There were always plenty of woods to hunt just a short distance from the beach. Mostly cottontail rabbits, ruffed grouse, and bobwhite quail were our main quarry. They were everywhere. Some of the best hunting of that type I'll ever recall- but, I wanted to hunt deer. They were also there, but not like up north.

We later moved to upstate New York during my sophomore year of high school...Spencer Lake to be exact. The town was so small, it said... "Welcome to Spencer" on both sides of the sign! Spencer-Van Etten was the high school we attended when we weren't out in the woods somewhere. That's when my deer hunting education really kicked in.

Yes, wildlife biology was my favorite subject. In fact, it was hard to keep me out of the woods, even to go to school. One class I did enjoy though, was drivers education. Dale Weston was my favorite teacher because he loved to drive around all the back roads looking for deer and turkeys, all the while teaching us to *drive slowly, always watch for four-legged pedestrians,* and to *parallel park* wherever there was a good view of an open field! We didn't have a GPS in those days, but we always had binoculars!

After school, there was more scouting to do. I would go by myself if I had to, but my preference was to go with my good friend Harry Van De Mark. Harry and his wife, Elaine were my heros back then. As husband and wife, they were National Archery Champions and loved the outdoors as much as I did. I would randomly stop by their house (conveniently around 4:00 p.m.) for a visit, and before you knew it, Harry and I were off in his truck with two pairs of binoculars to go scout for big bucks on his favorite hillside. This was always my favorite way to scout because we'd always see some big bucks while I got to listen to some of Harry's exciting hunting stories!

My brothers and I practiced shooting our bows every day after school and all weekend long. With our old Browning recurves, we could hit each others arrows inside a paper cup at twenty-five yards all day long. No sights, no releases, no range finders, just a bow and arrow. But, when I had a deer in front of me, all bets were off! I educated buck after buck, shooting over their backs, under their bellies, in front or behind them, but never in the *"paper cup!"* With all that practicing, I guess I just had bad luck!

Now, this wasn't the case for my best friend, Kevin Brown. He had the opposite luck than what I had been blessed with.

It was 5:00 a.m. opening morning of archery season one year, we all spent the night at *Brown's Cabin.* We were all ready to leave to go hunt...except for Kevin. He seemed to have misplaced his bow, the same bow he's had for the last 15 years! He asked his Mom if she had seen it anywhere. Eleanor said, "It's in the barn where you left it last year!"

Kevin blew the dust off and shook out the cobwebs, then borrowed some arrows and broadheads of mine, and was ready to hunt. Off we went in different directions with plans to meet back late in the morning for breakfast.

Upon returning to the cabin, we swapped stories of the morning adventures and none of us got a deer. I missed one though! Then Kevin said, "Look over there in the tree!" He had an eight pointer hanging up! "Look where I hit him," he said. So I did. I couldn't find where he had shot this deer. There was no hole! He went on to explain...

He said, the deer came down the logging trail and stopped right in front of him at fifteen yards. Kevin took careful aim at the bucks vital zone, then proceeded to shoot right over his back! The buck ran off, jumped over a barbed wire fence, stumbled over a rock wall, fell and broke his neck...and his neck was broken- *I checked!* That's the kind of luck I don't have, but Kevin does! Not to take anything away, he is truly one of the best deer hunters I have ever known to this day. I heard he just got a new bow last year! I wonder if it came with arrows?

Down the road a bit...three or four years down the road, I was hunting near our home when my luck would finally change. It wouldn't change without putting up a struggle, but it did change.

My step brother Tim, and I went to a wooded ridge that bordered a large ragweed field with a small pond. I love to hunt these type of ridges. Even the road we lived on was named "Ridge Road!" I picked a random tree along the field edge and Tim moved further on down to the other end. I put a few drops of "Doe in heat" urine ten yards out in front of my stand. As the sun was going down, a seven point buck came walking slowly in, but unalarmed while being drawn to the scent drops. I was shaking like a leaf, as I usually do when a deer's in front of me. The curious buck walked right under my tree. At a very steep angle, I drew back the arrow and aimed for the heart. I let go of the bowstring and just about fell out of the tree! My binoculars had gotten in the way, tangled on my bow string, and yanked my neck forward as my arrow landed harmlessly in the dirt at his feet! *I was livid!* I subconsciously screamed, *"I'll never get a deer!"* Then the buck stopped in the open field and looked back. I put another arrow on the string, started to draw back, hesitated, remembered to pull my binoculars safely behind me, and made a perfect shot! I couldn't believe my eyes, ***"I got one!"***

Tim walked up just seconds later as the buck was still thrashing in the bushes. I guess he forgot what tree I was in because he stopped directly beneath the branch I was sitting on without noticing me. Tim heard the bucks horns raking the bush, and thought he'd try to call this buck in! He quickly got out his rattling antlers and grunt tube and went to work. I watched him for one or two unsuccessful minutes until long after the thrashing subsided.

With the most perplexed and mischievous smerk on my face, I finally said, "HEY! ...What are you doing down there?" Tim looked up with a surprised, then irritated sneer and said, "Shhhhhh, there's a buck over there in the bushes!" I said, "I know, I just shot him!" I won't say what he said to me next but, being a good sport, he was happy for me and helped me drag my first buck with a bow out of the woods. He still hasn't got me back for that one yet!

Since that first teaser buck, it just got harder and harder to ever get another. I had a big one picked out that lived on our back 40, who had a huge rub on a cedar tree. Year after year he rubbed that same ol' tree and each year the rubs only got bigger! One day I went to check on his rubs and saw a big fresh ground scrape he just opened up right next to it. So, I hustled back to the house, grabbed a treestand, ran back and set it up. It was only one o'clock in the afternoon and I was going to wait all day if I had to.

I got up in the stand, began hoisting my bow up, when suddenly, here came the buck walking casually to check on his scrape! As I expected, he was *very* big! I pulled on that rope as fast as I could, but he was too close. I had to stop and wait because as he came down the hill, he was now at eye level with me.

The big heavy ten-pointer stopped as he noticed my bow suspended mid hoist, slowly spinning on the string. I was hoping it would hypnotize him, then I could do what ever I pleased...but it didn't work out that way. The buck swapped ends and disappeared back into the briared rose hip thickets, abandoning his scrape forever.

My natural affinity with big scrapes has always had a way of elevating my enthusiasm when I would run across one. My excitement level would soar at the sight of a really fresh one. This is what I would primarily look for each time I was in the woods deciding on a stand location.

One morning while scouting, I found a few fresh new scrapes together and thought I'd give it a try for the afternoon hunt. I set up my stand, but on my way out of the woods, I found another scrape. This time, it was the big one! At almost five feet across, the ground was so recently raked, you could smell the fresh earth and the tarsal laced urine! Extra large hoof prints in the center of the scrape stamped this bucks interdigital signature.

I retrieved my stand, relocated it at this new scrape, and didn't leave. At around 4:00, a big wide twenty inch ten-point buck snuck in from behind me. I watched him as he carefully approached the scrape location. Still at 15 yards behind me, he did something I've never seen a buck do before and will probably never see again. He rolled on his back for ten minutes or more as if to scratch himself like a dog would do. Maybe he found something stinky to use as cologne or was just scratching his back. All four legs were pointing straight up to expose his white underside; an angle not often viewed on a live deer. *What a show!*

Then he got up, looked around cautiously, and continued toward the scrape. I wondered what trick he would have up his sleeve to get out of this one, as I was sure he'd offer an opportunity for a lethal shot.

Coming through the last of the thick cover, the buck was at just five yards away. "Just two more steps," I said under my breath, and he'd be in the open. I held full draw, and two more steps he took...at which point I released the arrow!

The heartshot buck ran about fifty yards and tipped over in plain sight. I was ecstatic! I just shot the biggest buck on our property! Until just seconds later...when the **biggest buck on our property** walked up to me with two does and showed me his massive set of antlers! He was a 170 inch chocolate-horned monster! He freshened up *his* scrape, stood in front of me at less than ten yards away, showing me every profile of his amazing set of antlers. This lasted for the rest of the day it seemed, then he simply walked away with the does...unaware (or unconcerned) of my presence just 14 feet above!

Regardless of my frustrations that afternoon, I was delighted as could be with the wide rack ten-pointer I had on the ground, but to this day, I've never seen a bigger buck on our Upstate New York property than that second one!

For the first time in my young hunting life, I asked myself a most puzzling question: "...Why *did* that happen the way it happened? Why didn't the *BIG* buck show up before the *smaller* one? Why couldn't I have shot *him*?"

Well, I'll tell you why. Because, just like all the other deer in this chapter, it was all part of a Grand Scheme, an "Insight" perhaps; lessons of a lurking phenomenon I would become all too familiar with later in my hunting life, and these were just... *"The Early Warning Signs!"*

"A little Birdie..."

NOW YOU SEE IT...!

*O*ne of the greatest pleasures of bowhunting big whitetails in the Midwest is bringing a friend along who has never been there before. In this case, the friend was my stepbrother, Tim.

I had been hunting the Midwest for many years, going to every state you can name that is known for big bucks, telling Tim of each adventure and whetting his appetite for his own hunt. I'm not sure if he believed any of my big buck claims unless I had a picture to back up the story, which wasn't very often.

One year I decided to take Tim on his own deer hunt to Illinois, to see things for himself. One such "storybook buck" I told him about was on a lease I hunted the previous year in Brown County. I'm quite certain he thought I was exaggerating when I told him this deer would push the magic 200 inch mark!

I had a plan all worked out for us to set up on this giant bruiser and Tim would have as good a chance of getting a crack at him as I would, as long as the buck would *show up* as per the plan. The question was, would the buck be willing to cooperate?

We had our tree stands in hand as Tim followed me down the heavily wooded trail to where I thought would be *the* tree to set up in. The other stand would be across the ravine on a side hill within one hundred and fifty yards or less of stand number one.

After setting up the first stand and remaining quiet as possible, I whispered to Tim and pointed across the hill to show where I wanted to put stand number two. As I pointed, I explained how the buck we were after liked to use this ravine to travel from the tangled brushy creek bottom below, uphill to the lush grassy pastures and corn fields above. The area was covered with rubs of all sizes, as different bucks were homing in on the does that were feeding there late in the afternoon.

At around noon, the plan was to set up the second stand, then hunt all day and wait out *the big one*. As I continued whispering, I pointed to a particular shelf about three quarters of the way between the two stand locations where I had seen the buck the year before. Again, emphasizing on the truth of how big this buck really was. I don't doubt that Tim thought I may have been embellishing the description of this monarch buck just a little bit, when in the middle of my sentence...the massive monster arose from his bed while I was pointing right at him! It was almost as if I had somehow summoned this buck to magically appear before our very eyes!

Our jaws dropped to the ground! The buck stood there broadside, looking straight at us as if to say, "...See that Tim, he wasn't kidding, ***I'm absolutely huge!***" We didn't know what else to do but take in the view. Any second now he would exit stage left, and with no further hesitation, that's exactly what he did!

Standing there stupefied with the most ridiculous grimace on our faces we could possibly muster, I said, "Well Tim, now you see it...*and now you don't!*"

We knew a buck of this caliber didn't get that way by being dumb. I always say, "Big bucks make a living...*by living!*"

Tim would doubt my stories no more, as we both knew we would never see that gargantuan animal again. As for this hunt, that was a true statement; as for ever again? Well, I did see that buck one more time...

After that hunting season had ended, I spent countless hours over the next five months, trying to come up with a game plan on how to outsmart this savvy survivor with a sense of humor. Inventiveness eluded me and not one viable game plan was I able to conjure up. As hard as I tried, it was like my brain was in hibernation mode all winter.

Then sometime in April with the change of seasons upon us, I went out into the back yard to feed all the wild birds, as I do every morning. There's every kind of wild bird you can think of in my back yard including my favorite...the hummingbirds. This time however, I noticed how all the birds were already gathered, awaiting my arrival before I got there. Suddenly, it was like a lightbulb went off in my head! "A little birdie had told me a secret!"

I had suddenly formulated an infallible game plan on exactly how I would take this most witty super buck of all. I had it all figured out. All the years of feeding the wild birds in my backyard had finally paid off!

Bow season couldn't get here fast enough. Every angle of this covert operation was worked out in my mind as I rehearsed over and over how I would set my tree stand in the middle of the night and wait there in his own *"back yard"* for his return from the fields at first light. I had exact confirmation of where he liked to bed during daylight hours stored in my GPS, so all I had to do was check the wind before I picked which tree to shoot him from! Mental preparation would be key as this was going to be an all or nothing proposition once the buck came home to bed. Now if the calendar would just fast forward to my state of anticipation.

Sometime during the middle of summer, I received a phone call I also rehearsed, but hate to say...*"dreaded."* As luck would have it, I got the tragic news we had lost that particular Brown County lease, and depression quickly set in. I would not get the chance to implement my foolproof strategy and go after this once in a lifetime deer again. I was devastated.
Autumn eventually settled in. My multi-state deer hunt would go as scheduled including Illinois, but of corse not on my old Brown County lease. As I said earlier, I would see this buck one more time...

The hunting season came and went. Back home in Florida, I resumed my off season routine of feeding the wild birds in my backyard and having my morning cup of coffee on the deck while they fed. This gives me the perfect opportunity for one of my other favorite things besides hunting, and that's...*reading about hunting!*
While thumbing through one of my favorite magazines to gawk at some of last season's featured success photos, I turned the page and about fell out of my chair! I was staring at my Brown County Bruiser...in the pages of North American Whitetail magazine! *"No-o-o-o-o!"* That was part of *my* plan! My dream to be in a magazine holding up a 200 inch Whitetail Deer was just ripped out from underneath me!

Dejected to say the least, I finished my *mourning* coffee, threw another handful of seeds to the birds, and called Tim to commiserate. After seeing the article, Tim agreed it was him, the same enormous buck...and just to show I don't exaggerate, he scored 205 inches!

Two things are true: If you don't own the property you're hunting on, you're going to lose it someday. Secondly, if you find a giant buck on that property, you're going to lose it sooner!

Tim and my brother Tony were the only two people I've ever told about this tremendous deer. So, with my hat off to the person who got that incredible buck of a lifetime, a sincere "Congratulations" is in order! I have to wonder though, *"...Who was the little birdie that told you?"*

"Logness Monster!"

IT COMES IN MANY FORMS

*I*n a lighthearted, yet cynical attempt to humor myself, it's somewhat soothing to know I'm not the only one whose hunting life has been plagued by the infamous spirit that has been the central character of this book. Although I can honestly say, I'd be surprised if anyone can catch me at this stage of the game, it points out that it can literally happen to anyone, anywhere, and at anytime. Unfortunately, it usually does. Whenever I begin to tell someone a story of this subject matter, I'm quickly interrupted by the other person's similar recollection. They are always so surprised and relieved to hear that it's happened to someone beside themselves...*oh, if they only knew!*

---

*O*ne of the most unexpected surprises occurred while driving west on highway 108, cutting across the great state of Illinois from Carrollton to the Illinois River at Kampsville, then to continue up through Pike County on this beautiful October autumn afternoon.

Racing down the highway without a care, I was suddenly distracted by an intense, alert stare on my furry four legged passenger's face. My Black Lab, Gator, was suddenly "on point" and transfixed on an object up ahead a little way off into the distance.

Straining ahead to see what critter could possibly be commanding every ounce of my dog's attention, it was too early in the day for deer to be feeding on the lush roadside vegetation and too late in the day for pebble picking pheasants to be showing their one vulnerability to the hawks. I scanned left, then right...*nothing*. Finally noticing a dark figure ahead of us out in the water...I couldn't believe my eyes!

Gator had spotted the Logness Monster...***swimming up the Illinois River!*** With all eyes locked on to this mythical creature, we sped ahead to get a closer look.

At over 70 miles per hour and the river just ahead of us where the monster was swimming, I glanced forward to keep the vehicle on the road. Suddenly...*there was no road!* It ended and disappeared into the Illinois River! Brakes locked up, high-pitched squeals and smoke bellowing from all four tires, we came to a screeching halt with my poor puppy's head wedged against the windshield. With just inches to spare, we glanced down at the chilly waters edge...then each other. "Where did the road go?"

Unfamiliar to me, this was a ferry crossing road and we were about to *miss the boat* and go for a swim. That would have been fine for Gator- he wanted to go retrieve the Logness Monster for me! I just wanted to stay alive to hunt another day!

Right then and there, my hunt almost ended before it began, but not before snapping off a few quick pictures for the tabloids!

The ferry arrived shortly thereafter and my first ride across the Illinois River was an enlightening and dry one after all. But, what became of the Logness Monster? I wonder if he's still out there waiting to foil plans of other unsuspecting hunters. People ask me if I ever sent the pictures in to Star Magazine or The Inquirer, and I reply, "...It's an unmistakable case of *Scotoma*." Sometimes your eyes can simply play tricks on you...hence the spelling: "***Log*-ness!**"

My beautiful niece, Lexa, has her own form of voodoo she likes to impose on her Father's and my hunt each year. She sends her personal influence in picture form, by sketching a creative scene of hilarious events, depicting an exhibition of wacky arrow trajectories, resulting in a doomed hunt every time. We always get such a kick out of her sense of humor and her young imagination, but having never spent much time in the woods with us, how does she so accurately know so much, I wonder?

The next handful of chapters are some of the craziest stories of them all. It goes to show that it truly does come in many forms. Nonetheless bizarre, these are mostly condensed versions of much longer stories. Just the same, theirs's no reason to drag out the inevitable endings. The facts and final outcome remain the same...truly, a baffling mystery!

INVISIBLE

Back in the days when you could easily draw an Arizona archery elk license, it was just a matter of picking which unit you wanted to hunt. We're not going back too many years either; the coveted Arizona elk tag is at a higher demand than any other I know. I used to take it for granted when I'd draw a unit 6B or unit 7 license, but how times have changed in what seems like the blink of an eye!

If I would have only known back then how I would come to appreciate that tag today, I would have hunted a lot harder and a lot smarter. At least I was wise enough to show up one day ahead of time, so I could scout new areas and set up camp!

The second year I hunted Arizona, something quite ironic occurred. It was one day before opening day of archery season. I was driving very slowly down one of the orange and brown colored dirt roads in unit 7, before it was split into units A & B. I was looking for signs of life, wildlife to be exact. It was the middle of the day when most savvy critters were in their safe havens waiting for daylight to dissipate, as most hunted animals only travel in the cover of near darkness. I wasn't expecting to see anything other than sign or tracks, rubs and wallows...that sort of thing.

Gazing ahead through the dry timber, I thought how the conditions were very conducive to hunting here in Unit 7. The woods had plenty of trees for shade and cover, but open enough to see long distances. I drove from one watering hole, (or "tanks" as we call them in elk country) to another looking for big oversized bull elk tracks and rubs.

As I was scanning out over the hood of my truck, a mule deer came into view in the far off distance and was walking perpendicular to the dirt road, a couple hundred yards or so ahead of me. I stopped the truck and raised the binoculars to zoom in on him. My eyes almost popped right out of their sockets!

This muley buck was enormous! I've seen many-a-mule deer in my days, but this one was the topper of em' all! A typical 4x4 mainframe, with eye guards, 30 inch-plus spread, big deep forks...*perfection on hooves!* I'd have to guess this buck would go into the mid to upper 190's, as he was absolutely enormous! The fact that he was still in velvet made him look even more impressive.

I pulled the truck up to where the buck would eventually cross the road, then shut it off. He quartered toward the truck as if I weren't even there, and casually continued forward. I quietly got out and stood at the left front corner of the vehicle. Standing straight up, I was not trying too hard to conceal anything other than the puzzled look on my face, considering the fact that there was a big white truck in the middle of the orange dirt road! The giant buck continued on, closer and closer. I remained silent and still while the buck seemed oblivious, sort of sleep walking, continuing his casual stroll through the forest. He then walked right in front of me at ten yards as if I was...*invisible!*

Completely dumbfounded, I drew back my *"invisible bow"* and put my *"invisible pin"* right on his vitals as he stopped for a moment to watch my eyes begin to cross. He let me ponder that ironic moment and think about it for a while. I had no choice. All I could do was *think* about it, because it was one day before the season opened!

The buck decided he's not done with me yet as he eased forward to give me a few more *shot options!* How about quartering forward at eight yards? Not close enough? Seven yards! Too close? Out to ten yards now and still showing me the perfect shot angle!

I released my *invisible arrow* and imagined a perfectly placed shot zeroing in on its mark. Then nausea set in, because the buck just stood there looking at me. At that point I realized there was nothing I could do to fast forward the hands of time to the following day. I had to just stand there and take it, as the muley buck of my dreams now took his sweet ol' time fading into the distance...like a ghost! I watched that incredible deer until he was too far away for even my eight power binoculars to decipher; evaporating into the hazy-grey pine forest.

Hovering in my now bewildered state, I thought I would never see that deer again. Was I ever wrong! I see him at night in my deer hunting dreams, I see him every time I'm in a pine forest in Arizona, I see him every time I'm watching a Mule deer hunt on the Outdoor Channel, and I see him every time I draw back my *invisible* bow.

Isn't it amazing it seems, when you have no chance of putting your tag on that once in a lifetime deer, he's right there in front of you for the taking? Why is that? Would *this* ever happen if it was opening day of deer season...or the middle of deer season...or even the very last day of deer season? Of course not, because that's when *they* become..."*Invisible!!!*"

MISGUIDED

*H*ave you ever been on a guided hunt? I usually do a *"do it yourself"* type of hunt, only because that's what I'm used to or can afford. Most professional guides I know are a true asset to have, especially if you've never been to the area you're planning to hunt. Their vast knowledge of the local area and the scouting time they can save you is invaluable when you only have that one vacation week a year in which to hunt. I know many guides, and some are the best woodsmen and hunters I've ever met. I always give the lion's share of the credit of a successfully guided hunt to the guide.

I've mainly hired outfitters just to pack me in to a wilderness area where I can do a self-guided hunt, like I do in the Gila Mountains of New Mexico. I've done this type of hunt many times, and it has always been a very special experience. I always look forward to getting on one of the horses, then trail riding for the better part of a day to get to my wilderness destination. It's amazing to see how much weight those mules can carry on their backs, uphill all the way, without complaining a bit. And, a good mountain trained horse is a pleasure to ride. I never seem to get one of those horses! I always pick the horse that no one else wants to ride. I guess I feel sorry for him or her, then I soon find out why no one else want to ride that one. *My* horse has usually never seen a mountain before, much less had a passenger on their back for that matter. If a bear or a mountain lion has crossed the trail within the last 24 hours, *my* horse goes ballistic, throws me for a loop and takes off running. If thunder or lightning strikes, it's like they opened the chute at the Albuquerque Rodeo, and again I go flying. I wouldn't want to hang on for that eight-second ride if I could. Nobody else's horse reacts to any of that, *they're all mountain trained!* One day I had to tell my horse, "If you throw me off one more time, you'll have to walk all the way to camp by yourself!"

One particular year, I put in my application for a coveted New Mexico high demand bull elk license and once again I did not draw a tag. I had to locate and purchase a very expensive landowner tag if I wanted to hunt elk that season. That costed me more money than I could comfortably afford, but I did it anyway. I had no other choice and cringed at the thought of missing an elk season.

I found a licensed New Mexico outfitter and explained what my objective was. He had access to a landowner tag and would gladly sell it to me as long as I agreed to hire him to pack me into the wilderness area for separate fee. I agreed and sent him a check for the license amount and "pack-in" deposit.

Upon arrival at our predetermined location, I met Parley Hall in person: Large hat, big rodeo belt buckle the size of a dinner plate, and pointy boots. He sure looked the part all right...a real cowboy!

Promptly after initial greetings, Parley asked me for the balance of the money but said he couldn't pack me in on this particular day as planned because his partner didn't show up to get the horses ready. He said he would do it the following day.

I waited two more days, when late in the morning, he showed up to pack me in with *no horses!* Again, he said his partner didn't show up or was sick; come to find out, he and his partner were in a rodeo together. However, he was still insistent on asking for the money. I asked him where all the horses were? He promised to be there with horses the next day if I would just give him all the money now. I said I'd have the balance when he was ready to pack me in.

The following day he showed up with a big empty horse trailer and again, no horses or partner. He attempted to convince me to pay him in full and that's when I said, **"Show me the horses!"** Now, I've missed the first four days of my ten day hunt and I still haven't seen a packhorse one!

At this point I was sure I was dealing with a true *"rodeo clown!"* Have you ever heard the saying, "Big hat, no cattle?" The same goes for horses, and after driving 1500 miles from Florida to find this out, I gave Parley Hall the "boot!" I was left in the middle of New Mexico with no plan, not much time left, and no place to hunt!

I resorted to the areas national forestry maps and old dirt roads in an attempt to salvage my hunt, but all the elk seemed to be on private land. (How do they know the boundaries? Have the elk learned to read these maps too?)

I ran into another couple of hunters who were doing exactly the same. We asked each other if we were having any luck. JP Rodriguez and his son, Roman, were not seeing much either and invited me to their camp for dinner to commiserate. JP said his wife, Letticia, had made some fresh Mexican food with red chile so I had to except *that* offer! Not being one to show up empty handed, I grabbed a Blackberry pie from Pie Town, right up the road, hoping for an invite to breakfast as well. It worked!

The guys were astonished with my story and couldn't believe a licensed outfitter would do this to a client after having worked all year to save the money, and driving all the way from Florida to fulfill a sacred dream.

The hunt turned out to be a bust, as time quickly ran out on me. The only elk I saw were just on the other side of a private property sign nailed to a pine tree. I don't think I saw one elk on public land, but to this day I'm still friends with JP and his whole family. He sends me dried chiles in the mail every year as long as Letticia gets after him to remember to do so, and I always stop in for a visit and a Mexican cooking class when I'm in their neck of the woods!

As for the slick-talking outfitter I hired to pack me in? To no avail, I filed a complaint against him with the state of New Mexico, but never got satisfaction. He received a reprimand by the state officials, but never offered my money back for his behavior. I often wonder how many other people got *lassoed* in with his *trick riding*?

In the most bizarre and unexpected way to date, I was duped into another failed hunt. At least I can now say with confidence..."This isn't my first rodeo!" But, I have to ask two remaining questions: "Was I just

simply *misguided?*" And..."Who was this *partner* that never showed up?" Could it have been...in the most unscrupulous form...?
"*...Naaaa!*"

THE BUCK STOPS HERE!

I remember the excitement of my first hunting trip to Wisconsin like it was yesterday. After leaving the warmer weather in Illinois, my good friend and well known Whitetail deer biologist, Steve Shea and I were heading north for some cooler weather and hopefully better deer movement.

The weather was definitely much cooler when we arrived, and it was obvious the deer were on the move. We couldn't wait to get in the woods. Steve's brother, Tommy, was there ahead of us and had some stands in place all ready to go.

After a cup of coffee and a quick breakfast, we went over the game plan. Now, it was time to make it happen.

We all walked in to the woods together and I was pointed to my treestand. I was a little skeptical about the location, but having never hunted there before, I didn't question and I really didn't care. I was just happy to be in the woods and invited along for the hunt. Steve and Tommy headed further back into the deeper cover of the Wisconsin hardwood forest. The leaves were crunchy and the air was cold and crisp with almost no wind, as I awaited the first deer sighting of the day.

A couple of uneventful hours went by without seeing a single doe. I was shivering alittle from the cold, but it was still very early in the morning. The grunt tube would provide the only form of entertainment as I blew a few notes just to break up the monotony, if nothing else. I had a feeling this stand wasn't going to produce, it just didn't have that lucky aura about it, yet I was quite content to be a guest amongst the squirrels and birds that were busy gathering food for the long, cold winter on the way.

Easing back into my warmest position, I suddenly heard the unmistakable sound of deer footsteps moving quickly in the dry autumn leaves! I got ready and took a closer look with the binoculars. It was a big shooter buck, and he was quartering downhill from behind me toward my shooting position. I could tell he was a perfect ten point with a huge body.

As he angled past me, he was a little too far to take a shot. I knew the deer was in a hurry to get somewhere, so I grabbed the grunt tube, already out, and made two or three perfectly pitched calls. The buck instantly turned and started up the slight incline in the direction of the call, right toward my stand. He looked alittle confused, I recall. Now within thirty yards, all he had to do was turn slightly broadside and the deal would be done!

The buck took a few more steps then stopped. He stood there for a second, then began to wrench his neck and look back downhill. I knew I would have no problem with this 30 yard shot, but before ever drawing my bowstring back, the buck all of a sudden...*just tipped over!* I did a double-take, thinking..."Wow, I didn't even shoot!"

The buck scrambled downhill a few more yards and lay there while I tried to figure out what had just happened. I put the binoculars back up to inspect the situation alittle closer, and noticed a spot of red on the deer's underside. Apparently, someone had already shot this buck I was about to shoot!

Other than scratching my head alittle, I sat very still for the next thirty minutes or so. Then lighter footsteps in the crunchy leaves revealed the rightful owner of the deer, in slow but meticulous pursuit. It was Steve in search of his buck.

I whistled to him to get his attention, as he detoured over to my location. I told him I saw his deer go down and pointed in the general direction. Climbing down out of my stand, Steve waited for me to walk him over to his trophy.

Upon seeing the big ten point on the ground, Steve replayed the events for me and revealed a perfect heartshot. *We were ecstatic!*

Steve's brother Tommy came walking up shortly after to join us, and was proud of his older brothers accomplishment. After some congratulatory high fives and hand shakes, the buck roughly scored around 140 inches and was Steve's biggest buck up to that date. I immediately gave Tommy huge credit with the "assist" as he did his homework and put his brother in the perfect location.

Being the consummate pro that he is, since then, Steve has taken much bigger deer than that one, but I'll never forget his excitement for having put his first Pope & Young'r in the books!

In a way, we all had a hand in taking this most memorable buck. I'll never forget it. How could I? *It was a bizarre!* Just when I thought I was going to get a sure shot and tag a big Wisconsin whitetail buck, something entirely mind boggling occurred to deflate my optimistic opportunity. I've never seen anything like that happen before or since. When that deer fell over without me ever letting go an arrow, all I knew was... *"The buck certainly did stop there!"* No question about that part of the equation. There's one quizzical note I had to contemplate, though.
"Did someone else also...*have a hand in it???*"

SO CLOSE, YET SO...*CLOSE*!

*I*t seems like just yesterday, while looking over a new piece of property to hunt in Illinois, it somehow reminded me of my trophy room at home: *"Undersized and full of questions!"*

I decided to hike lightly this particular day and carry as few items as possible, as this would be a quick scouting job on this small piece of land. With only my treestand in hand, I quietly snuck in on the downwind side of the property, careful not to spook any of the deer I knew were bedded nearby. I planned to hunt this woodlot later the same afternoon. After a quick look at the main bottleneck of this eighteen acre parcel, I decided I had found the perfect location to set up shop.

The only thing between me and where I wanted to hang this stand was a small creek merely five feet in width. As I approached the creek bed, a small buck caught my attention heading my way on the edge of a cut cornfield, bird dogging a hot doe. I froze to let him pass, which he did undisturbed. I realized, "This may be my lucky day!" as the buck walked past me at only twenty yards!

Eyeing the exact tree I wanted to set my tree stand in, I took a few more steps downhill to the edge of the creek. Just before I stepped into the water to go across, a large...no- *huge,* swollen-neck ten-point buck was trailing the same hot doe. This one *was* a shooter!

With his nose barely skimming the ground, he continued on the same path as the previous buck, but opted to take a detour and get a critically needed drink of water from the creek. He was walking straight at me as I crouched down and began to hug the creek bank I was standing on, helplessly hoping to conceal myself by hiding in plain sight.

He then came down the opposite bank and stopped, standing in the creek no less than four feet from me. I said, "***Feet***," not yards...*as in forty-eight inches!* Oblivious to my presence, apparently, I had blended in perfectly.

When I realized how close he was, I wondered if this was really happening or if it was an illusion...or a dream, as I counted the points on his rack. Eight, nine, ten I recall, as he lowered his head, adorning his heavy, extra-wide, ivory tipped rack. Then I began counting the whiskers on his face.

Steadily slurping his fill of cold, refreshing water, he suddenly jerked his head up and looked me right in the eyes and *froze*, as the water dripped from his chin back into the creek. My eyes quickly squinted to conceal the identifying white. Once again, he calmly lowered his head to continue his drink.

I watched him with my eyes forced to one side, as he seemed at ease with the situation. Being at arms length, I was literally close enough to reach out and touch him. This is something I've always wanted to do but didn't want to spoil the moment, as this was truly an amazing one!

Questions soon began racing through my mind and nerves became unraveled, wondering how this rut crazed buck would react if he figured out I was of the human kind. I imagined his long dagger-like tines impaling my ribcage, inflicting lethal damage; something this buck was easily capable of doing during this *"edgy"* time of the year.

Nose forward, looking straight up at me one last time, he temporarily held pose. The deep stare made me wonder if he knew I was there all along. With more important things on his mind, he turned up the bank and off he went, continuing his trek in search of a new romance.

Exhaling a sigh of relief, I thought, "Have fun my friend," as I was doing exactly the same!

I remained crouched in amazement, still awestruck by the event, as the inevitable questions began entering my mind.

Recalling how the deer just walked right under the exact tree I chose to hunt from, then strolled casually to within whispering distance of me, I wondered..."Would he have gotten that close if I hadn't left my bow back in the truck?" Certainly not! I probably wouldn't even have seen him if I had my *bow* in my hand instead of a *tree stand*. What a thrill to be so close to a majestic animal such as that! The memory of this grand buck is etched into my brain with the clearest visual definition of a mature Odocoileus Virginianus as if he were actually on my wall. I wouldn't have traded it for anything...*given the choice*!

And speaking of..."Why wasn't I given the choice? Why didn't I have a say in the matter?" Could it be that...being a *memory* instead of a wallhanging was this bucks plan all along?

As I survey the sparse landscape of my personal trophy room at home...my answer mysteriously appears!

A WILD MOOSE CHASE
(The Tale of the Bull!)

*I*t took me a number of years to bury the ax and commit to another guided hunt after the fiasco I had in New Mexico with the "Rodeo Clown" outfitter. A moose no less, would be the quarry of choice, with hopes of also redeeming my Alaskan Dream Hunt.

British Colombia, I figured, would change my luck. A Canadian moose hunt was exactly what I needed to do, and 2010 was the year to do it. I did all the necessary homework including finding the right area in which to achieve my humble goal of a fifty inch bull.

The Omineca Mountains was the area I found to suit all purposes and now I needed to find a reputable outfitter. I researched a number of outfitters in the area and settled on Sel Nella with Southern Woodsman Outfitters. I told him my objective of the hunt and began working out the details. He said he had just the area in mind for me, and was known for big bulls. He promised me I would be the first and only hunter in this camp in three years and would have the place all to myself. If I shot a bull early enough on this eight day hunt, I could hunt a Mountain Goat for just a trophy fee. It all sounded good to me and the hunt was booked!

I would be picked up at 6:00 a.m. on September 25 at the Esthers Inn Hotel in Prince George and a two hour ($1500.00) float plane ride would deliver me to the cabin at the pristine camp in the Omineca Mountains we agreed on. Even though the generic contract stated a "wall tent" was the standard accommodations, I was told I would be staying in a cabin. Not that I cared, a wall tent would fit my idea of a wilderness hunt much better anyhow.

The driver for the outfitter, a very pleasant *"mate"* from Australia, was at the hotel right on time and there was no hesitation getting on our way...since we had a seven hour drive on bumpy Canadian dirt roads to get to the float plane to fly to the hunting area. ***Surprise!*** A seven hour drive??? That was considered "day one" of my eight day hunt!

Another hunting party from Madrid, Spain was also along for the ride. Felix, David (Da-veed), and Jose were three of the most excited hunters I'd ever met. Traveling all the way from Spain to hunt moose together as a group had their spirits soaring! They all had humorous personalities and interesting lives and stories to share.

Roughly after halfway through our seven hour trek on bumpy dirt roads, I mentioned to the other guys that this unannounced road trip was a surprise to me and I was under the impression we would be flying from Prince George to the hunt area. They also were not aware of this extra 4-wheel drive adventure, but it didn't seem to bother them too much as we were enjoying each others company, stories, and the scenery. I told them, "The scenery would have been much nicer from the air!"

At this point of our tour, the driver asked which of the three Spanish hunters would like to be split from the group to hunt in a separate camp? The tone of the conversation went nearly silent, with only a few whispery Spanish words barely audible. Since I speak alittle Spanish, I understood the concern immediately. None of the three wanted to hunt in separate camps. They were all here together and wanted to hunt together, according to plan. The driver explained that the outfitter told him to split the group up because he didn't have accommodations ready for three hunters in one camp. He said it would only be for a day or two, then the odd hunter would be reunited with the group. They scratched their heads with confused looks on their faces. When they turned to me for consult, I muttered the first Spanish phrase the guys would hear me speak. I simply said, "This is Cocka de Toro!" (translated in English... "Shit of the Bull" or simply put, *"...Bullshit!"* They were relieved to hear their native language but confused at the same time. They said, "You speak *es*-Spanish?" I said, "*es*-Si!" They asked me if this splitting of the group was normal and I said, "Absolutely not. If you booked together to hunt as a group you should hunt as a group!"

The remainder of the drive was low-toned discussion of unexpected surprises to come and how to handle this one in particular. Felix volunteered to split off from the group and hunt with me in my camp. There was only one problem with that...I was supposed to be the only one in my camp! Now we would have two people hunting in my exclusive (small) area for the same animals. Felix and I agreed we had absolutely no problem with each other's company, but this was not what we bought into.

Upon reaching the destination where the float plane would pick us up, the rain and cloudy low ceiling had us wondering if we were going to be socked in for the day or make it out to our hunt area. Then we heard the distant engine rumble coming in through the fog as it eerily reminded me of a ghost from the *"Alaskan past."*

The plane descended through the fog then touched down on the glassy Canadian lake and taxied in to the dock. The pilot/outfitter, debarked the aircraft and immediately got out his folder to square up with everyone on the monetary balance of the hunt. Barely a "Hello," he encouraged a sense of urgency as he handed me an itemized piece of paper with the balance due at the bottom of the page. As the rain continued, I looked at the paper and didn't recognize the balance to be what I had expected. It was off by a large amount...*and not in my favor!* As the raindrops dotted the invoice, I thought, "Wow, this is a convenient time to sort out details!" Well, it needed to be handled, as Sel seemed to grow more irritated with my audit. I said, "I'm sorry, I know this is untimely, but it has to be done." When I refigured the math and showed him what I thought was the correct number, he immediately pulled out another invoice from his folder with the correct amount! I shook my head and said, *"Hmmm*...convenient is right!" That one seemed to match a little better, and with a sidewards glance I squared up with him. Felix showed me his invoice that seemed to be off by quite a margin as well. All three Spaniards were also charged an extra $200.00 *each* for a box of bullets supplied by the outfitter due to strict international laws not allowing them to travel with such items. I told him we'd talk more about it later as we were hurried into the plane.

Off we went into the wild grey yonder; Felix in the copilot seat and I... cramped in the back seat with all the gear stuffed all around me, some on top of me. I felt like cargo instead of a passenger.

My $1500.00 plane ride to the remote, pristine wilderness area took all of exactly seven minutes from takeoff to touchdown and I thought, "Stay positive"...as I've said before,"Some of the best hunts start out this way!" However, this time I was struggling to get comfortable with the idea as Felix was also charged $1500.00 for the same brief flight.

The float plane taxied to the edge of the lake, Felix and I got out. No cabin! A couple of dilapidated wall tents (ours dated 1968!) and a tarp-covered, makeshift lean-tu was home for the next week. Scattered around the rough cut lumber tables was a variety of leftover food from the previous group of three hunters. The previous group??? I was supposed to be the first hunter in this camp in the last three years!

The outfitter promptly left to continue his flying duties as Felix and I met the two hired guides and inspected the camp. The guides were friendly and pleasant, but the camp left much to be desired. For example ...*food!* The outfitter took off in the floatplane without leaving any food! When I thought about it, we never loaded any in the first place.

The two guides promptly offered us a hot cup of coffee that had been brewing over the fire. Felix and I both accepted and attempted to fix it to our preferred taste. Only one problem with that...there was no sugar or cream! Luckily I remembered I had an emergency stash in my duffle bag I saved from the hotel room the night before. Then, as I retrieved it to the table, the two guides were excited! They hadn't had cream and sugar in their coffee in weeks. I asked why not if that's the way they take their coffee, and they snidely replied, "Well...uhh" was the only answer returned.

The following morning was the first attempt at trying to find a moose. It was a cold, late September morning, and prime time to hunt rutting moose in this area. Still dark out, Felix and his guide headed south while my guide Jack, and I, headed north. We trekked through the Canadian brush towards the distant wood line a half mile from camp. There, we would let out the first of many sultry, seductive cow moose calls in hopes of luring a big, mature bull moose into bow range.

We waited for an answer or even the snapping of a twig to indicate we were being acknowledged. Call after call, only silence was returned. Moving further away from camp with each calling session brought no better results.

We decided to return to camp for breakfast and try again in the afternoon. Upon our arrival back, Felix and his guide were already there with a small campfire and a fresh pot of coffee. We exchanged stories of our uneventful morning hunt, then I went into the tent to change out of my hunting clothes.

Moments later, Felix followed me into the tent and seemed to have a perplexed look on his face. I said, "So Felix, you didn't see any moose this morning either?" "Nothing came into dee camp," he answered somberly in his heavily Spanish-laced accent. "What do you mean...nothing came into the camp?" I replied. Felix pointed to a mound of grass not more than forty yards from our tent. He said, "That is where I hunted *dees* morning." I said, "You mean, you never left camp?" "Si' Da-veed, we never left *da* camp. We called for *dee* moose...no moose come to us...so we go back to *haf* more cafe. *Dot waas eet!*"

"Oh no...you better sit down Felix, we need to talk about this outfitter and our hunt right now, OK?" I told Felix about other *"misguided"* hunts I've been on and how I now have a trained eye for this sort of thing, and unfortunately I'm having a very bad feeling about this one too.

Felix looked around the tent for a moment or two and said, "Da-veed, in *es*-Spain we *haf* one saying: When you are in a bullfight with *dee* bull, you never know what will happen until *da* tail of *dee* bull passes!"

I thought about that for a moment and said, "You're right! I don't know what you just said, but you're right! Can you explain that to me in English?" I asked. Felix went on to elaborate... "In *es*-Spain we *haf* bullfights, and when *dee* bull is in *da* ring and coming *ofter* you...you hope *dot dees* bull will not *keel* you. First *dee* horns of *dee* bull go past you, then *da* head, then *da* neck, *da* back, and so on. You do not know the outcome of *dees* fight until *da* tail of *dee* bull passes you!"

"OK, I get it now. You are staying positive until the end. That's great and I appreciate the story, I need to stay positive too." (But, in the back of my mind, I suspected the bull's tail had already passed.)

Day three came and went just as quietly as the second day had. The only difference was that Felix and his guide had ventured a couple hundred yards away from camp instead of the usual thirty-five yards. Didn't matter though, no moose were seen or heard by either of us. I just couldn't understand this when most Canadian residents talk about moose in their backyards! I was determined to get to the bottom of this.

I asked my guide what might be the problem and or the solution since this was a noted "Mecca" for big bulls in the 55-60 inch range. When I told him about the other broken promises by our outfitter thus far, including the seven hour drive, the money problem at the dock, the "*cabin*," the food, (or lack there of) and how I was supposed to be the first and only hunter here in three years, and how this affects him as well, he began to listen very closely. I told Jack that I felt bad for him since a good part of his paycheck hinges on the outcome of the hunt. If I were to get a bull moose on the ground, it would require alot of extra work on his part to help me skin, quarter, and pack the animal back to camp; hence a hefty tip for all the effort involved.

Then the conversation got real interesting as he began to voice some of his own frustrations with this outfitter as well. It suddenly occurred to him that his paycheck ***was*** sabotaged just like my hunt. He then told me that the outfitter was baiting for wolves and Grizzly bears in the area for the previous and future hunters. Then corrected himself and said, "Well, just baiting wolves...*it's illegal to bait grizzlies in Canada!*"

Consequently, with three mature grizzlies in the area, he hadn't seen a moose in weeks. I said, "*Ahhh,* so that's how you do it in B.C....*A?*"

The outfitter eventually returned to pick up Felix to be reunited with his group. A small amount of perishable food was left for camp with no ice or refrigeration, which promptly soured. I had to fish in the lake for trout for supper. A new bucket of moose meat was also left to be put out for the "wolves" though. With Jack standing next to me, I asked the outfitter about the "taker" moose he saw right outside of camp just prior to my arrival, that the guides knew nothing about. He quickly replied that the moose were everywhere but they move around a lot. I told him I have put on countless miles in the last three days and not seen as much as a fresh track and could he just point me in the general direction of where he saw the bull he spoke of. In a defensive tone he replied, "Don't get Friday-*itis* on me...you have plenty of time left." I said, "I appreciate the help and encouraging words from a highly-paid, seasoned northern woodsman such as yourself!" At that point, he and Felix left, hopefully for greener pastures.

I continued to hunt day in and day out to exhaust all possible excuses, and maybe, just maybe, a lone moose would come out of hiding for me.

But, it was not to be. With three large, hungry, mature Grizzly bears in the immediate area, there were no moose to be found. Nature, influenced by my outfitter would prevail, as the wolves and bears would keep the moose scattered at least until after I left the providence. My hunt was over before it ever began as I realized I was on *"...A Wild Moose Chase!"*

On day eight I was supposed to be picked up at first light and returned to Prince George to catch my flight back to the States. However, the outfitter didn't show-up until sometime after lunch. I reminded him that according to our contract I was supposed to be delivered back to Prince George by 8:00 a.m. and had booked connecting flights accordingly. He denied that part of our written agreement and continued breaking down most of the camp for another hour or so.

After seven minutes of flying, we were back at the original pick up/drop-off point. I told the outfitter I assumed I would be driven seven hours back to Prince George, not flown as promised? No reply. I asked for a copy of my contract and at that point, the outfitter exploded with physical threats while wrestling to get his jacket off! He didn't make good on that promise either and I left in the truck with my guide who quit his job, vowing never to work for this outfitter again.

Upon a final conversation with Felix, I told him how I appreciated his positive attitude as we were now heading back to our native countries. I will save his encouraging story for future reference, although I'm sure it will be a long time before I do another guided moose hunt. Yet another dream adventure somehow crushed by circumstances beyond my control. As for this hunt, I knew the tail of the bull had passed many days ago. Unfortunately now, we were left with only my original Spanish words: **"*Cocka de Toro!*"**...what comes from under...*"Dee* tail of *dee* bull!"

IN FACT...STRANGER THAN FICTION!

*I*n this later chapter, I still try to decipher the matter of this book's puzzling link to reality. Although most of us have had similar experiences in the woods that tend to work against us, there's a few chosen individuals who have been blessed with the opposite arrangement!

My dear friends, Don Reich and his wife Yvonne, who live Southern California are like family to me. Over the many years we've known each other, I can hardly remember a time going to their house for a visit and not walking away with a door prize! It's either a bottle of Don's homemade prickly pear wine or something hand made by either of the two that you'll never forget. They are the most generous and giving people I've ever known.

Don and I have had more fun together, hunting sheep on Santa Cruz Island off the California coast or hunting Wild Boar in central California with our hilarious friends from Paso Robles, Marvin and Greg Blackburn. On one such hog hunt, I recall Don laughing uncontrollably as he witnessed a comical wrestling match between two grown men, over who got to sleep in the top bunk of the camper! The two grown men (or should I say,"overgrown boys") were Marvin and myself. It was all in good fun, and I really didn't care where I slept, but I don't think Marvin will throw my sleeping bag off the top bunk again! When we woke up the next morning...we were still laughing!

At age 77, Don has more hunting stories than Fred Bear himself, and between the two of us, we can go on for days. That's why I like to stay with them at their home when I travel back to California to visit. It's not to save money on a hotel, it's because that way I don't have to leave when it gets late, and we can just keep on talking until the *wee hours*. Reconvening at the breakfast table, it's like we didn't skip a beat, we just pick up the story where we left off the night before!

Years ago, Don introduced me to one of his lifelong hunting buddies, Freddy Troncoso, founder of Golden Key Futura Archery Products in Montrose, Colorado. On my first ever hunt to Colorado, Freddy and his wife Eva, took me in me like long lost family and treated me to a wonderful home cooked Mexican Carne Asada dinner with home made flour tortillas, guacamole, and salsa! As far as I was concerned, from that point on we were friends for life too!

Freddy graciously pointed me and a hunting buddy around the Southern Colorado wilderness. He just seemed to know exactly what the elk were doing at any particular time. Maybe this was due to years of experience, but I believe he had a gift few of us possess. This led me to my first archery elk, a beautiful 5x5 bull!

Freddy came to visit my camp one evening during our hunt and I was extremely happy to return the dinner favor in the form of fresh elk steaks, as we talked about some of his adventures with the famous Howard Hill. We also talked about some of his and Don's earlier hunts back in the day as well. They all had their share of hunts go wrong too, but they had many go right! My first ever archery elk hunt in Colorado went very right, thanks to Freddy. I'll never forget his knowledge, sincerity, and generosity on that unforgettable adventure! If you were a friend of Don's, you were a friend of Freddy's too, and I'm forever grateful to have gotten to know him.

Don grew up hunting with his father. From an early age and for over forty years they hunted together. In the early days, he was an excited eight year old boy following his father in search of a buck. In those last few years, it was his Dad following *him*.

His father was one of the very few hand selected individuals who had a mystic perception, sort of a spiritual intuition that transcended ordinary understanding of the outdoors to an equal, yet opposite level of what the rest of us have been blessed with. *I can vouch for that!*

Many times Don recalls, when they were deer hunting together, his father would stop for no known reason, look around without saying a word to him, turn and move in a completely new direction. Seconds later, only to spot a mule deer buck bedded just yards away totally unaware of their presence! There were no tracks, no noise or clues whatsoever, he just knew the buck was there. How? No one knows. Not even his Dad!

Later, when Don questioned his Father about these occurrences, he admitted himself he didn't know, understand, or even recognize it when it happened. But, on rare occasions when his Dad did hunt alone, the same thing would occur on a regular basis. Again, he would shoot the deer at close range without the deer ever knowing he was there. He said he felt *"Invisible"* so to speak. I can easily say that I was not blessed with this gift, unless it was the day before the season opened! (Hence the chapter by the same name!)

Another unusual encounter Don would talk about, occurred while he was on a mule deer hunt on the famous Kaibab Plateau on the North Rim of the Grand Canyon in Arizona.

A rifle shot rang out from somewhere over the plateau. Later while walking along the rim, Don stumbled upon a lone hunter dragging out a mule deer buck. This was no ordinary hunter, though. This man was a Native American Indian from the Hopi Tribe of Northern Arizona.

A very interesting conversation ensued as the general greetings continued. When asked how he shot this buck, the Hopi said he hadn't shot it at all! But, Don had heard him fire the shot. Well, in fact, he heard *a shot*, but not by this man.

The Hopi said he also heard the shot as well, and watched as another hunter walked over to take a look at the buck he had just taken. Upon seeing the buck, it apparently had undergone a transformation we're all too familiar with, known as "ground shrinkage!" The hunter just turned and walked away from the lifeless animal, apparently not well enough impressed.

When the Native American explained to Don that the forest was like his sacred place of church and how this deer was now in the category of "Spiritual gifts," he went on to elaborate how the deer now belonged to him.

Don pondered the theory of "Situation Ethics" as would a Fish & Game officer. However, the Hopi believed that, (in his own words) "You don't *hunt* the deer...the deer are *sent* to you!" The Hopi interpreted this as his own harvest and was very proud and content! Don and I both thought this was most interesting.

Well, the deer are certainly not *sent* to me, nor do I possess the *"power"* of Don's father. Actually, quite the other way around. But, I've hunted with Don enough to know that he rarely comes home empty-handed!

"In fact..." I believe Don may not recognize the same gift his Father was blessed with. Because, *"Stranger than fiction"* and just like his Father, Don has the *"power"* too!"

CONCLUSION & FINAL THOUGHTS

    Could it be anything but a coincidence what occurred on my final hunt just prior to this book going to print? After three years of applying for the coveted Iowa nonresident archery deer license, I finally drew my long-awaited tag. I was very fortunate to have friends of the family, (now, more like family) invite my brother Tony and I to bowhunt their family farm.
    Upon greetings, I was given a tour of the property. The corn was cut, the deer were in the woods (*where they belong*) and I was eager to start zeroing in a giant Iowa whitetail.
    With the possibility of getting a crack at a two hundred inch non-typical buck known to be roaming the farm, the vision of his trail-cam photo flashed repeatedly in my mind as I looked for signs that would tip me off to his secret hiding place.
    Tracks don't lie; they can tell you the size of the deer, which direction he is going, how long ago he was there, how fast he was moving, and if he was alone or with others. Eventually, I would locate his *elk-sized* hoof print, and set up within a stones throw from his preferred core area and bedding ground. The size of this deer's track was the largest I have ever seen in the woods, ***in- my- life*** and I believed he would tip the scale at well over the three-hundred pound mark. The area was scattered with big rubs that were three and a half feet up on six-inch cedar trees! I was very eager to get a first hand look at him. I set up in an all or nothing location; if I would be lucky enough to get a look at him, I would also get a shot at him as well!
    On the fourth day of the hunt, my brother Tony shot a beautiful ten-point buck, and the land owner shot a gorgeous thirteen-point buck on the same day. This was great news, except- as luck would have it, they both ran and dropped right in the big non-typical's bedroom!

The commotion of four guys dragging two deer out of the woods instantly dismissed any hope of ever seeing this great buck on this farm during this hunt...so, off I went to Wisconsin.

When I arrived at my favorite stomping grounds, the first thing I noticed was that the corn had been already cut down here as well. That was a first, and very encouraging!

I only had a few days to hunt Wisconsin, but having filled my doe tag the previous season, I had my "Earn-a-buck" tag ready to go.

It didn't take long to find an absolute monster buck since I knew the area quite well by now, as my HD video camera recorded the giant, white-racked, extra wide eleven-point working a scrape. I relocated my stand immediately and set up down wind accordingly.

For the next two days, the wind had switched 180 degrees out of the Southeast. I could only watch from another distant stand as the tall, wide eleven-point with a split G-2 worked his scrape right on schedule.

Finally, on the last morning of my hunt, the wind changed back out of the Northwest and I slipped into my stand well before daylight.

Around 7:00am, sitting quite comfortably and cozy in my most promising treestand, I caught a glimpse of a big buck moving through the mixed conifer trees in the direction of my setup. The hazy lighting on this particular morning was unusually eerie...almost spooky, as I brought the binoculars up to get a more accurate look and make sure this was the targeted deer I had hoped would show up. Happily confirmed, he stepped into the expected opening while I drew back my bow for an easy 18 yard shot.

As I centered my 20 yard pin on his vitals, a smaller buck stepped right in front of him like a silhouette...*and stopped!* I figured the big buck would not tolerate this smaller fellow anywhere near his primary scrape, but I was wrong! This smaller buck *had* to be his son, because he stood there for the longest time without a concern. I continued drawn back, but the little buck wouldn't get out of the way for a shot. He was like a shield! When he finally did move on, the giant buck moved step for step with him...simultaneously like a shadow! Slyly, the targeted buck walked away into the timber, giving me no chance of a shot. Was he teaching his son a new *"Divine Antlervention"* deer trick? And speaking of *"deer tricks"*... I had one last afternoon hunt remaining, although I wasn't sure I would make it back from the Doctors's office in time to get in the woods. As luck would have it, I was bitten on the back by a dreaded *"Deer Tick!"* I didn't pay too much attention to the nagging pain for a while for the simple reason I didn't know it was a tick bite.

Just a few days earlier in Iowa, I had a treestand set up in the one specie of trees I *painfully* dread, the thorny Black Locust tree. It was the only tree in exactly the right spot from which to hunt the two-hundred inch non-typical I was after, which turned out to be exactly the wrong spot! However, the treestand had to be removed before I went on to Wisconsin, so back up in this precarious tree I went, one last time. Upon completing the task, I had painful puncture wounds all over my body from the subtle poison administered by the numerous needle-like thorns that protrude from every inch of this specie of tree. All irritations went away except for the *one* on my back. It only got worse by the day. By the time the Doctor got to examine the problem, the tick had drawn a baseball-size, black & blue bullseye which I could not see in the mirror, and I was already having muscular and joint pain. I was treated with a short round of powerful antibiotics which I inhaled and quickly and got back out in the woods for the final afternoon hunt.

The hunt conditions were again, *ideal!* However, the big eleven-point didn't show himself, but a beautiful ten-point did. I grunted him into bow range and made a perfect 20 yard shot...*hunt over!*

Upon returning to Florida, content with a nice big rack and a cooler full of fresh venison, I received a phone call from the Wisconsin D.N.R.

My deer tested positive for C.W.D.! (deer's version of mad cow disease) This is not a problem for human consumption as far as anyone knows, it's said to be non-transferable, but the State of Florida Fish & Wildlife sure didn't like the idea of it being in the State of Florida and wanted to confiscate, incinerate, and eradicate it! The County Health Department also called to *encourage* me to relinquish the meat. The problem was, I didn't have it. I took it to the local butcher shop to have it all turned into hamburger, (who was also contacted by the authorities, forced to close down and clean all their equipment with harsh and expensive chemicals). I offered to pay all damages and personally help clean everything, but I don't think that gesture eased anyone's sentiments at the butcher shop.

So, I'm back in Florida with no venison, a bad case of Lyme Disease, and a cleaver-waving butcher mad as hell at me!

Pondering the whole mess, it's a painful irony to think I could have my life passion taken away...and all this trouble from one little tick! I figured it would all end someday with one mighty bite from a Grizzly Bear in Alaska or a Cape buffalo attack in Africa...but that would be too poetic for me. I can hardly wait to see what happens next year!

I know of so many people with incredible stories of a "Grand Distraction" that occurred in the final moments of the hunt, allowing the ***big one*** to get away. Some tales are truly unbelievable, but I don't doubt a single one...I believe them all!

On a serious note, during the 2008 Wisconsin archery deer season, my brother Tony had just such a distraction happen to him! After going the extra mile to locate a tree stand on the highest ridge top, far away from all other activity, a huge 160 class monster ten-point buck came walking under his treestand at 8:15 in the morning. Tony waited for the perfect moment, drew back the bowstring, grunted to stop the buck, (which he did stop) and missed the big ten-point at only eleven yards for no known reason. (Or, was it an eleven-point at only ten yards?) Either one would be a chip shot for his ability level; he's an impeccable shot with a bow.

Come to find out later that morning, the mystery meddling had occurred at exactly the same time, ***to the minute***, of our Father passing away halfway across the country in Pennsylvania! I know there's always a sign of the soul being released...or *"sent free!"* Was my Fathers' sign in the form of a deer? I think that would suit him just fine, while in retrospect, I know my brother feels the same. We never saw that buck again, nor will we forget the significance of that hunt.

Have you ever heard of an airplane making an emergency landing in your wilderness camp the day before the hunt that took nine years to draw a tag for began? I have! That was after scouting the area all summer long and locating seven giant bull elk in the immediate vicinity. No need to say they all disappeared; the hunt was over before it ever began! I call this, *"Instant Antlervention!"*

My friend Chris Lorea was hunting elk in Montana with a friend of ours, Chris Koreski, when he called in a beautiful 5x5 bull elk to within easy bow range of their set up. Chris' mechanical release had a mind of its own and decided to malfunction at about mid draw with the bull standing broadside at just fifteen yards, looking right at him. Upon drawing halfway back, not only did the release decide *when* to release, (the arrow arcing out to only ten yards) Chris' right hand recoiled backward, punching himself right in the mouth, nearly knocking himself out! Talk about adding "injury to insult!" The bull *and* the release remain wild and free somewhere in the mountains of Montana!

My first antelope buck I attempted to take years ago was an easy seventeen yard shot. Yet my four wheel Jennings Arrowstar, the fastest bow back in the day, still wasn't quite fast enough to outperform the guardian spirit of *"Divine Antlervention"*...even at that distance! The Pronghorn buck was standing broadside right in front of a water tank, yet upon release, he somehow managed to be magically wisked six feet straight up in the air and out of harms way, avoiding my near fatal ambush! The heavy Easton 2216 aluminum arrow struck the metal water tank with tremendous force and echoed a resonating...**"Bong-G-G!!!"** It was so loud, it reminded me of the Liberty Bell! *Actually*...just like the Liberty Bell, because it rang "Freedom" for that lucky buck! Bob Fromme was with me on that hunt, and to this day, we jokingly refer to this as a *"Well-* placed shot*!"*

On the same hunting trip, we traveled a little further north to Montana to hunt elk near West Yellowstone in the Hebgen Lake area. This region is known for its vast beauty and great hunting, but I couldn't forget one other thing Hebgen Lake is famous for. Long before I was even born, on August 17, 1959, a magnitude 7.5 earthquake "rocked" the local landscape like never before. It caused eighty-million tons of boulders to cascade down the mountainside and devastate the valley.

In the back of my mind, I thought, "Wouldn't that be just my luck to be drawn back on a monster bull..."

Bob and I woke up one morning and got out of our tents to start our day. It was a crisp, cool September morning. The first order of business was to sound off a locating bugle to see if any nearby elk would answer. They didn't! No response came back other than a faint echo off the mountain, so we continued on with the camp duties. Standing outside the tent while brushing my teeth in my long underwear, a bull elk snuck up behind us and sauntered right into our camp! I believe he walked right between our two tents. Apparently, he heard the bugle and did not respond vocally, but came to us within minutes. We thought he was going to join us for breakfast! The bull noticed neither of us were within scrambling distance of our bows, and seemed very comfortable being our guest.

Unable to resist the temptation, Bob grabbed the grunt tube and bugled at him to see what he would do. From only ten yards away, the bull's nervous response was to urinate all over our camp gear, then he exploded off the mountain with the rumble and fury of the 1959 earthquake! Dumbfounded, I was very thankful for the experience, as we stood there in our long underwear laughing with a mouth full of bubbly toothpaste!

The stories go on and on and on. Is it any wonder that,"*The Big One that got away*" is the main topic of conversation among hunting parties whenever we gather for any occasion at all? How about the evening before opening day of deer season when we attend the wild game dinners to celebrate the start of a new hunting season and reminisce over last years "*Shoulda had-em*" bucks? That's when we question the wisdom of making room in the freezer! Better yet, how about the evening *of* opening day at the local pub when all the new stories, pitiful excuses, and *sobering* beers are eagerly swopped! I know I've told my share of tall tales at the famous McAnns Bar & Grill in Van Etten, New York on that particular day, with all the wive's making fun in the background with their arms outstretched wide, saying, "Yeah, yeah, he was *this* big...*giggle, giggle!*"

Everyone I talk to about this subject has their own story of the "Once in a lifetime" giant buck that miraculously eluded a certain fate! Yet, I often wonder..."Why is it, this situation keeps happening over and over again?" Year after year, hunt after hunt, this phenomenon keeps re-hatching itself into different shapes and forms. Blunders just seem to continue with *Metamucil-like* regularity. What is "buck fever," anyway? No one has ever been able to accurately explain that to me yet. At least with this kind of luck, I get to hunt the whole season!

As we come to a close, I have to ask a few simple remaining questions: "Is someone trying to tell me something? Is somebody trying to get me to quit hunting and take up photography or gardening...or maybe cooking perhaps???" No, because you need to have something to cook! Photography would seem to make more sense to me. I could take pictures of the deer eating all the prize vegetables in my garden!

Well, I'm not going to surrender to the Big Buck Gods' persuasive behavior. I've been hunting this long...why give up now? I'm going to continue chasing my life long dream- my bowhunting quest to someday take that two hundred inch monster buck of a lifetime if it kills me!!!

Then again, I better be careful what I wish for...*you never know who might be listening!*

The End